D0962127

An Introduction to the Borderline Conditions

An Introduction to the Borderline Conditions

William N. Goldstein, M.D.

Jason Aronson, Inc.
Northvale, New Jersey
London

10 9 8 7 6 5 4 3 2 1

Library of Congress Cataloging in Publication Data

Goldstein, William N.
    An introduction to the borderline conditions

    Bibliography: p. 219
    Includes index.
    1. Personality, Disorders of. I. Title.
[DNLM: 1. Personality Disorders. WM 190 G624i]
RC554.G65   1985   616.89   85-9018
ISBN 0-87668-900-4

Manufactured in the United States of America

This book is dedicated to
Gladys and Ed

CONTENTS

PREFACE

The term *borderline personality* remains a controversial and confusing one in psychiatry today. A group of patients, initially appearing neurotic and analyzable, proved highly resistant to the psychoanalytic process. As psychoanalysts treated this group of patients, they wrote descriptive and psychodynamic accounts that detailed the difficulties these patients presented. Different diagnostic labels were assigned, with varying descriptions and theoretical conceptualizations. This diversity made it difficult for the psychiatric community to reach a consensus on a precise definition for the borderline personality. The work of Kernberg, beginning in 1967, provided an integration and synthesis of earlier writings, plus a unified and comprehensive framework for description, definition, and understanding.

In recent years the term *borderline*, initially confined to psychoanalytic use, has achieved wider application within the general psychiatric community. The tools of psychiatric research have been applied toward establishing a group of characteristic "borderline" symptoms, easily defined, reliable, and valid. With the publication of *DSM-III* (American Psychiatric Association 1980), "borderline personality" made its way into the official psychiatric nomenclature. Currently the term is widely used in both psychoanalytic and psychiatric circles, although the emphases of these two groups differ.

This book provides an ego psychological approach to

borderline conditions, focusing on diagnostic, psychodynamic, and therapeutic issues. The evolution of the term *borderline* is presented to clarify its current uses. A major goal of the book is to transmit an in-depth yet simplified understanding of the different uses of the term today This book, based in part on fourteen years of hospital experience, nine of which included intense involvement with teaching psychiatry residents and medical students, is written for psychiatry residents, psychology students, psychiatric social workers, and other mental health professionals. In addition, the book can be a useful reference for more experienced therapists, as well as all those who want a psychodynamic overview of the borderline personality, and a correlation of the ego psychological approach with more descriptive ones.

To provide general background material on ego psychology, Part One focuses on the ego functions thought to be most relevant to the conception of the borderline individual. Introductory discussion of other ego functions, the id, and the superego, as well as a psychodynamic classification of psychopathology, is included.

Part Two discusses diagnosis and psychodynamics. First the early psychoanalytic writings thought to be most relevant to current conceptualizations of borderline conditions are reviewed. These include the work of Zilboorg, Hoch and Polatin, Bychowsky, Stern, Deutsch, Knight, and Frosch. Kernberg's monumental work is then presented. An ego psychological diagnostic approach, based on Kernberg's contribution, is outlined. This approach provides a contemporary, generally accepted summary of the psychodynamic concept of borderline psychopathology. Recent research is examined and compared with the more psychodynamic work, and *DSM-III* is critiqued. The possibility of using the dynamically oriented, ego psychological diagnostic approach within a research paradigm is explored. Other valuable contributors to the psychodynamic approach to borderline conditions include Meissner; Abend, Porder, and Willick; Rinsley and Masterson; Adler and Buie; and Gunderson. Their work is reviewed in Part Two and compared with that of Kernberg and the ego psychological diagnostic approach.

Part Three presents an overview of differential diagnosis, with special attention given to the narcissistic personality and schizophrenia. The relationship of narcissistic and borderline personalities is explored. The contributions of Kohut and Kernberg are reviewed, and related to the *DSM-III* definition of the narcissistic personality. The influential systems for the diagnosis of schizophrenia are reviewed to clarify the differential diagnosis of this disorder and the borderline conditions.

The treatment of borderline conditions is presented in Part Four. The borderline group consists of a wide variety of individuals, with different personalities and behaviors. An ego psychological approach enables one to classify these individuals as borderline in terms of their underlying characteristic profile of ego strengths and ego weaknesses. Six cases illustrate the variations among borderline individuals and their common underlying ego profiles. Through these cases, ego psychological diagnosis is compared with other approaches. The book concludes with a general overview of psychotherapy, classified into four types: psychoanalysis, analytically oriented psychotherapy, dynamically oriented psychotherapy, and supportive psychotherapy. Treatment of the borderline patient is discussed in accordance with each of these classifications.

ACKNOWLEDGMENTS

I would like to thank Karin, Matthew, and Lauren for their patience, understanding, and support. I would also like to thank Mrs. Flora Paoli for her constant availability and her outstanding typing skills.

PART ONE

Ego Psychology

CHAPTER 1

An Ego Function Approach

An effective way of both describing and understanding patients is through the study of ego functions. This approach aids in achieving diagnostic clarity and conceptual understanding, in therapeutic assessment, and in determining prognosis. It can be thought of as a bridge between descriptive and dynamic psychiatry, in that the ego functions can be examined totally descriptively or can be viewed as an aid to dynamic understanding. The ego function approach should stand alongside the mental status examination as a basic tool for precise and early assessment of any patient.

Freud's structural model (1923) differentiates the id, the ego, and the superego. These three structures are not entities in themselves; rather, they are hypothetical constructs that help explain the workings of the mind and human behavior. They are psychological, not biological, constructs. The id, present at birth, is conceptualized initially as an undifferentiated pool of drive energy, out of which the libidinal and aggressive instinctual drives rapidly emerge. With time these two instinctual drives are tamed or neutralized, and this neutralized energy is used to build the ego. Thus, the ego emerges from the id in a gradual and ongoing process, one that is well consolidated by age 3. Once formed, the ego becomes the chief mediator between the individual and the external world. It is the executive agency of the mind, continually interrelating, influencing, and being influenced by the instinctual drives, the superego (once that structure is formed), and the external world. All action takes place through the ego.

Freud (1940) later described the ego as having a number of principal characteristics. Anna Freud (1936) and Hartmann (1939) were among the first to list and describe various functions of the ego. More recently, Beres (1956) and Bellak (1958) conceptualized seven ego functions:

1. Relation to reality
   a. Adaptation to reality
   b. Reality testing
   c. Sense of reality
2. Regulation and control of drives
3. Object relations
4. Thought processes
5. Defensive functions
6. Autonomous functions
7. Synthetic-integrative function

Bellak (1970) and Bellak and Myers (1975) added several other ego functions: judgment, adaptive regression in the service of the ego, stimulus barrier, and mastery-competence.

Regardless of the classification of ego functions employed, one can then take an "ego inventory" and focus on specific ego strengths and specific ego weaknesses of the patient. This "ego inventory" can be thought of as a detailed description of the individual. A focus on the components of the superego—the conscience and the ego ideal—along with the libidinal and aggressive drives (the id) can supplement the ego inventory and help provide an even fuller assessment. Although this latter focus is useful, the "ego inventory" is sufficient in itself to establish a differential diagnosis among the three major groupings of psychopathology: the neurotic, the borderline, and the psychotic. This book will emphasize an ego psychological approach, and Part One will provide background for this approach. In the descriptions of the various ego functions, there will be an attempt to be simplistic and concrete. Although clearly there is much subtlety, complexity, overlap, and debate regarding the various ego functions, for our purposes, simplicity will be emphasized.

The six ego functions focused on when dealing with borderline patients are:

1. Functions relating to reality
   a. Reality testing
   b. Sense of reality
   c. Adaptation to reality
2. Impulse control and frustration tolerance
3. Thought processes
4. Interpersonal relations
5. Functions relating to the representational world: self and object representations
6. Defense mechanisms

The other ego functions that Bellak stresses, to which a briefer look will be afforded, include:

1. Judgment
2. Adaptive regression in the service of the ego
3. Stimulus barrier
4. Autonomous functions
5. Synthesis-integration

CHAPTER 2

The Ego Functions

Functions Relating to Reality

As in Bellak's original description (1958), reality functions will be broken down into three components: reality testing, sense of reality, and adaptation to reality.

REALITY TESTING

This is the ego function most assessed when considering the diagnosis of psychosis. In fact, psychosis has often been defined as a defect in reality testing. There are at least two ways of conceptualizing disturbances in reality testing. The first way, more commonly used, expresses global defects; it defines impaired reality testing as the inability to distinguish internal from external stimuli, or as the inability to tell what is occurring within one's mind from what is occurring in the outer world. This dysfunction in reality testing can be related to the concept of defective ego boundaries, as described by Federn (1952). Ego boundaries, in Federn's concept, are actually better understood

as self boundaries. The inability to differentiate self representations (or images) from object relationships (or images) is
intimately related to this definition of defective reality testing.
Developmentally, most would trace this defect to difficulties in
separating from the mother at the completion of the symbiotic
phase of development, as described by Mahler (Mahler, Pine,
and Bergman 1975). Delusions and hallucinations are the best
examples of defects in this aspect of reality testing.

The second way of describing impaired reality testing,
much more subtle and common, is related to the distortion of
present-day reality by infantile fantasies and infantile self and
object representations. This type of defect to some extent is
universal. Psychoanalysis is helpful in lessening this kind of
"distortion," yet it is almost impossible to eliminate entirely.

An example is provided by a 33-year-old woman who,
whenever confronted with a neutral or ambiguous message
from a friend or acquaintance, interpreted the message to
mean that the person did not like her. An infantile self
representation of herself as bad and unlikeable caused her to
feel others also viewed her this way. This distortion occurred
only when there was some ambiguity or stress.

A second example involves a 22-year-old man who, whenever there was ambiguity, felt that others were trying to take
advantage of him. An infantile object representation of a
significant other meeting his own needs at this young man's
expense caused him to perceive current reality that way. He had
these feelings only in very ambiguous situations or when under
stress.

A third example is provided by a 28-year-old man, of
considerable professional abilities, who, whenever he began to
become intimately involved with a woman, gradually came to
feel that the woman was beginning to see him as insignificant,
unskilled, ineffective, and sexually incompetent. He was fearful
that she might embarrass him and became convinced that she
wanted to end the relationship. At the same time, he viewed his
rivals for her affection as especially accomplished, powerful,
masculine individuals against whom he had no competitive
chance. This young man, at times of increasing intimacy,
invoked an infantile self representation of himself as little,

ineffective, easily hurt, and vulnerable. Correspondingly, he invoked an infantile object representation of others (based on his father) as all-powerful men who might disapprove and retaliate if he pursued his affections with the young woman (mother substitute).

This second kind of reality distortion is somewhat benign and occurs in neurotic as well as more troubled individuals. It is the first kind of reality impairment, the inability to distinguish internal from external stimuli, that is more specific to psychotic and borderline individuals. The psychotic shows major impairment in this area, either constantly demonstrating distortions in reality testing or continually mobilizing to prevent these reality distortions from surfacing. The borderline patient, in contrast, has a vulnerability, rather than a major impairment, in this area. In day-to-day functioning the borderline patient maintains reality testing without a constant expenditure of energy but remains vulnerable and sensitive to reversible regressions in reality testing under stress.

SENSE OF REALITY

An intact sense of reality is shown by the ability to experience one's self and body, along with external events, as real and familiar. This ability differs from reality testing in the emphasis on experience and feeling. Confused body images, feelings of estrangement, derealization, depersonalization, and *déjà vu* phenomena are common examples of defects in the sense of reality.

It is common for individuals to experience difficulty with the sense of reality while maintaining reality testing. Frosch (1964) distinguishes what he terms the psychotic character from the psychotic proper on the basis of such selective disturbances. Frosch's psychotic character experiences frequent impairments in the sense of reality, and in what Frosch calls the relationship to reality, while basically maintaining reality testing. Frosch's patients do, however, experience reversible regressions in reality testing under stress. Periodic disturbances in the sense of reality are not confined to more disturbed

people, occurring to some degree in many neurotic and so-
called normal individuals.

ADAPTATION TO REALITY

Adaptation to reality is basically a measure of how one copes
with and relates to the external world. There are some individuals who adapt effectively despite obvious impairments in
other ego functions, such as reality testing. Thus, adaptation to
reality is an important function to examine in patients who
struggle with impairments in reality testing.

The story is told of a psychiatrist who saw an individual
whom he had previously treated for a considerable time. The
patient was walking across the street in the business district of a
large city. The psychiatrist approached the ex-patient and
politely asked how he was doing. The patient replied that he felt
fine, that he was doing well, and that he was now a stockbroker
earning $120,000 a year. After departing, the psychiatrist
decided that he really wanted to ask his ex-patient one more
question. So he ran to catch up with him and inquired, "Do you
remember seven years ago, when you felt that there was an
influencing machine in your late grandmother's attic, with
gamma rays extending from the machine to your arms, legs,
and genitals, then extending back to the planet Uranus?" The
patient calmly replied, "Yes." The psychiatrist continued: "And
do you remember that you were certain that this machine was
exerting control over you and your body, influencing you to do
what your late grandmother wanted you to do?" Again the
patient calmly replied, "Yes." The psychiatrist then asked the
final question: "Whatever happened to that machine?" The
patient replied; "Nothing. It's still there, and it's still working.
Yet it no longer makes me anxious, and I don't tell anyone
about it anymore." The moral of the story is that some people
can have rather pronounced delusions or, sometimes, hallucinations in selected areas and still adapt adequately to reality.
Isolated delusions and hallucinations of this type—those that
do not greatly impair adaptation to reality, are most commonly
found in very chronic schizophrenic patients. These delusions

and hallucinations have usually existed for a number of years, have become ego syntonic, and no longer produce anxiety.

Impulse Control and Frustration Tolerance

Impulse control is the ability to cope with instinctual drives and impulses without acting. "Acting" here includes direct discharge of the drive or drive derivative, symptom formation, and regressive behavior. We are referring here mainly to the aggressive drive or aggressive drive derivatives, but the concept certainly also applies to the libidinal drive and libidinal drive derivatives. Frustration tolerance is a measure of how much additional frustration or anxiety an individual can tolerate before acting. This concept refers not to the total amount of frustration but, rather, to the additional load. Poor impulse control and poor frustration tolerance are concomitant, and in conjunction with them one finds an inability to delay, a demand for immediate gratification, and a proclivity to act out under stress. To make matters more difficult, these characteristics are frequently combined with a sense of entitlement.

In the extreme, difficulties in impulse control present themselves as episodes of explosive rage, directed to other people and resulting in bodily injury or even death. Slightly less severe is explosive rage in which inanimate objects are destroyed. Lesser but still obvious problems include childish tantrums and seemingly uncontrolled verbal abuse. More subtle defects include the tendency to excessive drug and alcohol use, uncontrolled gambling, accident proneness, and the tendency to leave work or interpersonal situations under stress. All these problems relate to the aggressive drive.

Extreme problems involving the libidinal drive are less common. Rape is an extreme example involving the loss of control of both drives. Repetitive masturbation and certain perversions represent other examples of loss of control of the libidinal drive. Premature ejaculation is an example of a subtle problem of this type.

Problems in impulse control and frustration tolerance are

common. They invariably are seen in borderline and psychotic individuals, but they also occur in many of the lower-level character disorders, in the addictions, and, to a lesser degree, in many of the neuroses.

Thought Processes

This ego function reflects the ability to think logically, coherently, abstractly, and intelligibly. The term *secondary process thinking* is used to describe goal-directed, logical, easily understood thinking, typically used by most adults. Primary process thinking, most often associated with schizophrenia but also typical of small children and of adult dreams, is a seemingly illogical and idiosyncratic way of thinking, yet has definite rules of its own. Primary process thinking is characterized by condensation, displacement, absence of negatives, absence of qualifiers, timelessness, mutually contradictory coexisting ideas, representation by allusion, and predicative identification. Whereas the normal person accepts identity only on the basis of identical subjects, the paleologician (schizophrenic), invoking the principle of predicative identification, accepts identity based on identical predicates (Arieti 1955). Thus, if two people are wearing identical shirts, they are assumed to be the same person; if two people or objects have like parts, they are assumed to be identical (*pars pro toto*).

The term *formal thought disorder* has been used to describe the difficulty in conceptual thinking that occurs when there is an intrusion of primary process thinking where secondary process ought to be employed. The term *thought disorder* was employed by Bleuler (1950) as characteristic of schizophrenia. For a time it was in vogue to focus on the patient's thinking pattern to see if a formal thought disorder could be demonstrated, thus justifying the diagnosis of schizophrenia. To aid in diagnosis, a number of systems classifying thought disorders arose. Oppenheimer (1971), discussing schizophrenia, describes in detail seven types of formal thought disorders. Four (desymbolization of the word, semantic shift, metonymic distortion, and neologism) are based on word use, and three (asyndesis, system shifting, and sham language) are based on sentence use. All these are based on the intrusion of primary process thinking into secondary process, and most rely heavily on the concept of predicative identification.

Several examples of thought disorders involving predicative identification may be useful. A middle-aged Jewish man, upon entering the office, said that he could sing better than Cantor Grazinnitski. When asked how he arrived at this idea, he said that on the way to the office, he passed a girl in a yellow dress. Yellow was the color of butter, and from butter, he went to better, and got the idea that he could sing better than the cantor. The predicates yellow, butter, and better were all equated via the primary process, enabling the patient to reach his conclusion. A second example is that of a young woman who felt that her psychiatrist, whenever he touched his glasses, was giving her signals to trust him. She arrived at this conclusion by noting the rust color of the psychiatrist's glasses and thinking of the term *trust*. A last example involves a middle-aged woman who, when another patient, during a community meeting, said, "Let's get to the point," leaped up in a very excited manner, shouting that she knew all about pointillism as a form of art. Here the term *point*, meant in one context, was placed in a totally different context because of the literal sound of the word. The words *point* and *pointillism* were equated in the primary process.

Recent psychiatric research (Pope and Lipinski 1978, Pope, Lipinski, Cohen, et al. 1980, Procci 1976) has indicated that the thought disorder is not necessarily pathognomonic for schizophrenia, particularly when comparing schizophrenia with manic-depressive illness. The presence of marked or frequent problems in conceptual thinking, however, is frequently associated with schizophrenia and certainly most often indicates some psychotic process. Brief reversible regressions in conceptual thinking, under stress or in unstructured situations, are generally thought to be characteristic of many borderline patients. Often the Rorschach test can demonstrate difficulties of this type that are not apparent during the clinical interview.

Interpersonal Relations

The terms *interpersonal relations* and *object relations* are often used interchangeably, despite definite technical differences in meaning. The term *interpersonal relations* will be used here to mean the personal interactions that actually take place between individuals, either in the present or in the past. In contrast, the term *object relations* denotes the internalized derivatives of these interactions. Object relations include object images (object representations) that are built up in the ego as the result of the way the individual has perceived, processed, and internalized past interpersonal experiences. Besides object images (object representations) *object relations* technically include self images (self representations). These self images are built up in the ego as a result of the way the individual has perceived, processed, and internalized his varying past conceptions of his self. Thus, interpersonal relations describes interactions, involvements, and experiences between individuals; object relations describes a state within the ego.

As we will discuss later, there is some controversy concerning the proper use of the terms *self* and *object representations*. The conceptualization just presented represents only one of a number of ways these terms are used. Although a listing of ego functions usually includes the term *object relations*, what is described frequently is more in accordance with interpersonal relations. Here, interpersonal relations will be listed as one ego function, describing the individual's typical relationships with other people. The self and object representations underlying these interpersonal relations will be detailed under a separate ego function, that relating to the representational world.

A mature interpersonal relationship is one in which the individual, in addition to attempting to gratify his own needs in the relationship, views the other as a separate person with his own special needs and desires. Emphasis is placed on helping the other person to gratify these special needs and desires, in addition to gratifying one's own needs. Respect, concern, and empathy are demonstrated in the relationship. There is always the quality of attempting to gratify one's own needs (at least unconsciously) in even the most mature interpersonal relationship, however. Relationships in which an individual seems interested only in the needs and desires of the other, to the exclusion of his own, often represent a kind of masochistic gratification (but gratification nonetheless).

A lower level of interpersonal relationship, common in borderline and psychotic individuals, is one in which the other person is basically "used" only to gratify one's own needs. Sometimes this kind of interpersonal relation appears more mature on the surface, because the individual, in meeting his own needs, may simultaneously gratify the needs of the other person. There is, however, no feeling for the other person as a separate individual with his own needs, no concern, no empathy, no depth of understanding, and no mutuality. Occasionally, individuals can form long-term relationships based on this more primitive kind of interpersonal relationship. An example is the marriage of a very passive, dependent individual, with a great need to be taken care of, to a dominant, parental individual with an equally great need to care for others. Another example is the relationship of a sadist to a masochist.

An even lower level of interpersonal relationship is one in which the individual distorts the characteristics of the other person in accordance with his own needs. Thus, if the need is to be taken care of, the other may be seen as strong and powerful, all evidence to the contrary being discarded. Relationships of this nature typically involve the use of very primitive defenses, along with at least subtle defects in reality testing. A still lower level of interpersonal relationship, basically confined to psychotic individuals, is one in which there is a loss of ego boundaries and a fusion with the other individual.

Functions Relating to the Representational World: Self and Object Representations

The representational world is another complex and controversial concept. As noted by Boesky (1983), there is much current disagreement about the usages of the terms *self representation* and *object representation*. Although self and object representations are listed here as an ego function, there is even disagreement about whether this is the case. Although Sandler and Rosenblatt (1962), Jacobson (1964), and Kernberg (1976a), among others, view these mental representations as part of the system ego, Boesky (1983) and others prefer to think of these representations as being formed by the interaction of ego, id, and superego and not residing in one system alone. Boesky notes theoretical difficulty with integrating the "representational" model with the structural theory. He views this integration as possible but difficult.

Despite these problems, the concepts of the representational world appear with great frequency in the literature, particularly with regard to borderline and psychotic individuals. Viewing self and object representations as part of the system ego simplifies, in a way, the concept of mental representations and seems the most helpful in understanding the literature on the borderline patient and the psychotic. This will be the view ascribed to in this book. The terms *self* and *object representations* will be used interchangeably with the terms *self* and *object images*.

The individual's representational world, as reflected in self and object representations, is directly related to the individual's object relations, as technically defined. In order to understand the ego functions relating to the representational world, one must understand the development of self and object representations. The abbreviated summary presented here will be basically that of Kernberg (1976a).

The newborn does not conceptualize self and object representations. As he begins to perceive the world around him and his caretakers as part of himself, however, he starts to experience fused self and object representations. When he begins to experience himself as separate from his caretakers, near the end of the first year of life, he begins to be able to differentiate self from object representations. This ability is synonymous with the capacity to test reality. According to Kernberg, even before the child has accomplished this developmental task—from early infancy on—he organizes his experiences according to whether they are perceived as positive or negative. Thus, early fused self-object representations are viewed as either all good or all bad. After self-object differentiation, early self representations and early object representations are separately linked with all good or all bad affect states. Thus, early self and object representations are generally viewed as either all good or all bad. It is typically not until the third year of life that self representations and object representations are associated with more complex affect states, related to the integration of all good and all bad affects. It is at this time that self and object representations become more complex.

In the healthy individual various self representations are gradually built up in the ego, coalesced, integrated, and synthesized into a stable, cohesive, and realistic sense of self. Concomitantly, various object representations are gradually formed in the ego, coalesced, integrated, and synthesized into a stable, cohesive, and realistic sense of others. These self and object representations provide the healthy individual with a stable, integrated identity.

Identity diffusion is a term that Erikson (1956) and Kernberg (1967, 1975) use to describe the lack of an integrated self concept and the lack of an integrated, stable concept of objects. Kernberg believes identity diffusion to be a core problem of the borderline individual. The individual with identity diffusion has not integrated good self images (representations) with bad self images (representations), but, instead, retains multiple, contradictory self images, some good and some bad. At one time, one self image is invoked; at another time, a different one. A meaningful, integrated image of the self is never formed. The same pattern occurs with objects. The individual's concept remains only a series of contradictory object images (representations), some good and some bad, with the attainment of meaningful, comprehensive images of others greatly lacking.

One result is the individual's inability to describe herself or significant others in a meaningful way. There is also a lack of temporal continuity regarding the self and others, along with an overall distortion of the perceptions of the self and others.

There is no stable, integrated identity. Clinically, this pattern is evident when an individual frequently shifts from group to group as she pursues an elusive identity. The term *chameleonlike* has been used to describe the tendency to become part of whatever group one has contact with, readily and rapidly shifting alliances whenever the next group presents itself. This trait is particularly striking when the different groups are antithetical. The individual is in constant search for and need for external organizations and groups, to which she easily adheres, in an attempt to attain a cohesive identity.

A level of organization somewhat higher than identity diffusion is the representational world often described for the narcissistic personality. Kohut's works (1966, 1968, 1971, 1972, 1977) and those of Kernberg (1970, 1974, 1975, 1976a, 1980a) are relevant here and will be detailed later. Here the self and object representations are stable and cohesive yet primitive, archaic, and unrealistic. Kohut views these archaic self and object representations as related to normally occurring infantile configurations that were never properly integrated. Kernberg, in contrast, sees them as the result of the development of very specific psychopathological structures. He believes that the self and object representations are distorted by a pathological fusion of the ideal self, the ideal object, and the actual self. At a level below identity diffusion is the representational world of the psychotic, characterized by at least an intermittent fusion of self and object representations and a corresponding blurring of reality.

Defense Mechanisms

Defense mechanisms, or defenses, refer to habitually occurring, unconscious mental phenomena employed by the ego to resolve conflict between the instinctual drives, the superego, and external reality. Defenses are developed basically to help hold in check unwanted aggressive or libidinal drives. Typically, an upsurge in aggressive or libidinal drive is opposed initially by the superego. The ego recognizes a danger, signals anxiety,

sometimes narcissistic defenses in day-to-day functioning but shows a tendency to use narcissistic defenses under stress. A typical borderline individual uses neurotic, immature, and borderline defenses in day-to-day functioning, displaying a proclivity for the borderline and, occasionally, narcissistic defenses under stress. Although the combination of defenses used in daily functioning in these two groups varies enormously, neither of these groups uses many mature defenses. In contrast, the typical neurotic uses mainly neurotic and mature defenses in day-to-day functioning, accentuating certain specific neurotic defenses under stress and occasionally using immature and borderline defenses. The healthiest group of patients uses a combination of neurotic and mature defenses, without any particular pattern of defensive regression under stress.

Individuals tend to repeat with great specificity their characteristic defensive patterns under stress. Thus, a young lawyer, who under the stress of his wife's leaving him, turned anger toward himself and became acutely depressed, became similarly depressed when passed over for a promotion at work. The postal worker who became paranoid when his boss became "too friendly" typically reacted that way in any close male relationship. The secretary who developed a fear of elevators after being sexually harassed by her employer in the office building developed a fear of being on the streets when she was the victim of sexual remarks by a group of construction workers. The principle is simple: If the stress is analogous, the individual will tend to act in the same way, using the same defensive pattern. Without psychotherapeutic intervention, this pattern often occurs repeatedly. In part, this principle explains recurrent suicide attempts, recurrent acting out, recurrent antisocial and criminal acts, and recurrent psychotic episodes. It also helps explain less pathological phenomena, such as recurrent neurotic symptoms, behavior traits, physical symptoms, and parapraxes.

The various specific defenses cited by Vaillant will not be described here. Excellent definitions are offered in Vaillant's article and are readily found elsewhere. Descriptions of the borderline defenses, however, are not as easily available. In addition, understanding some of them has proved to be a confusing process. A discussion of these specific defenses follows.

SPLITTING

There are a number of different definitions of the term *splitting* in the literature, as elaborated in an article by Lichtenberg and Slap (1973). With reference to the borderline personality, however, under the influence of Kernberg (1967, 1975), the term *splitting* has taken on a specific meaning: the tendency to view things (external objects) as either all good or all bad. There is often a concomitant tendency, under frustration, for complete reversals of the split: what was recently seen as all good suddenly is seen as all bad, or vice versa.

Primitive idealization, devaluation, and omnipotence are viewed as derivatives of splitting. Primitive idealization is the positive component of the split directed toward an external object. The object is viewed as all good not for any realistic reason, but only because the individual has the need or wish to see it as all good. Devaluation is the negative component of the split, directed toward an external object or toward the self. Omnipotence is the positive component of the split directed toward the self. A typical example is provided by a needy young man, hospitalized on an acute admission ward, who saw his therapist as all good and powerful while viewing the nursing staff as intrusive, provocative, and of little worth. When the therapist frustrated this patient by refusing him a weekend pass, the patient rapidly changed his mind, now viewing the therapist as sadistic and mean while approaching the nurses for maternal, loving care over the weekend. Another young man, when his previously "all good" therapist could not offer him a therapy hour before 7 A.M., quit therapy, stating that it was valueless anyway.

Although many individuals make rapid reversals from one side of the split to the other, particularly under stress, others tend to maintain their primitive idealizations and devaluations over long periods of time. Thus, one middle-aged woman, in treatment for over five years, varied little in overidealizing her therapist, even when there was great evidence to the contrary. An extreme example of this occurred when her 16-year-old son told her that her therapist had telephoned, had revealed supposedly confidential information about her, and had asked the son to act in accordance with this information. Rather than becoming annoyed at the therapist, or questioning her son about the reality of the event, the woman rationalized that her therapist was actually doing her a wonderful service by the telephone call.

PRIMITIVE DENIAL

Like *splitting*, the term *denial* has been used in a number of different ways. In the borderline patient the characteristic denial is of a primitive, global, and blatantly unrealistic nature, somewhat akin to both dissociation and splitting. In this defense, two events or facts are clearly remembered in consciousness, yet one is totally denied or ignored. Alternately, an event or fact is clearly remembered, but there is total denial of implications, consequences, and relevance. An example is provided by a 22-year-old man who, upon awakening from a coma in the intensive care unit of a hospital after his seventh suicide attempt, said, "Doc, I feel great! This will never happen again. I can absolutely assure you of that." The denial here is obviously global and has no realistic component. When questioned further, this young man could not elaborate on why he was so certain that "this" would never happen again. His only reason was that he was feeling very good at that moment. In contrast to this example, a more optimistic response was afforded by another young man, who also awoke from a coma caused by an overdose. This patient stated; "My God! I did that? That's very scary! Even though I feel better now, I had better do everything I can to try to understand why I would do something like that."

A more extreme example is provided by a 27-year-old woman who insisted on leaving the hospital prematurely after having stabbed herself in the chest with a curtain rod. The current admission was the sixth in three years for identical incidents. Currently she had "important matters" to take care of at home and saw no need to explore further what made her hurt herself repetitively. Because she was feeling so well now, she knew that this would not occur again, and she thus refused out-patient follow-up.

Patients who extensively use this primitive kind of denial, in conjunction with splitting, have a very difficult time staying in psychotherapy. Whenever the therapist frustrates the patient, the therapist is seen as all bad and the patient wants to leave treatment. Whenever the patient feels that he's doing well, he sees no need to continue therapy and again wants to leave. A patient who uses these two defenses (splitting and primitive denial) to too great an extent virtually cannot remain in treatment.

PROJECTIVE IDENTIFICATION

Projective identification provides the most conceptual difficulty of the borderline defenses. Like *splitting* and *denial*, the term is used in a number of different ways. Meissner (1980) elaborately reviewed the various uses of the term and concluded that it resulted in more confusion than clarification; he recommended that its use be abandoned. Abend, Porder, and Willick (1983), concurred, stating that *projective identification* was another poorly defined term with more potential for confusing clinical issues than for clarifying them. Yet this term remains in common use.

There are presently two common meanings of the term. The first is in accordance with the work of Kernberg (1967, 1975), who finds the term of great relevance when describing borderline patients. Kernberg's projective identification has two components: the first is projection itself, and the second is fusion of self and object images. Projection in the context of fusion of self and object images includes the characteristics that Kernberg attributes to projective identification. The concept applies to the borderline patient because this individual, in close interpersonal situations, tends to regress in reality testing;

that is, he tends to fuse self and object images. Thus, projections in these situations take on the characteristics of projective identification, such as the tendency for the individual to continue to experience the projected impulse as part of himself, and the need for the individual to control the object onto which the impulse is projected. Meissner, although he recommends abolishing the term, considers the meaning just described as the most useful. One might question Kernberg's explanation; it would seem simpler to state that projection and fusion of self and object images are occurring simultaneously than to use the term *projective identification.*

Another common use of the term *projective identification,* more complex than Kernberg's, is more in accordance with the Kleinians. The defense is described by Ogden (1979) as a process occurring in three steps. Step one involves the fantasy of projecting a part of oneself into another person, with that part controlling the person from within. The projected part is something the individual wishes to rid herself of, either because the part threatens to destroy the self from within or because the person feels the part is in danger of attack by other aspects of the self. A distinction is made between projective identification and projection here, in that in projective idenification the person projecting feels "at one with" the person into whom she has projected an aspect of herself. This feeling of oneness involves a blurring (or fusion) of self-object representations (or images). In contrast, in projection proper, the projector feels estranged from and threatened by the object of the projection.

Step two is an interpersonal interaction in which the projector actively pressures the recipient of the projection to think, feel, and act in accordance with the projection. According to Ogden, projective identification does not exist when there is no interaction of this nature.

Finally, in step three the projected feelings are reinternalized, after they have been psychologically processed by the recipient. The nature of the reinternalization process depends on the maturational level of the projector and can range from primitive types of introjection to mature forms of identification. Whatever the process, the reinternalization offers the projector the potential for attaining new ways of handling a set of feelings and fantasies that she could only wish to be rid of in the past. One can readily see how this conceptualization of projective identification can be applied to the psychotherapeutic process. In a recent presentation, Kernberg (1984) himself seems to define projective identification more in accordance with this second conceptualization.

An example of projective identification comes from a therapy session with a psychotic patient.* Mr. P, a 24-year-old man, was complaining that he was too weak to live and had poor eyesight. He stated, "I am my own worst enemy. I destroy things for myself. I need to be redeemed, revived. I need people to give me back what they have taken." Hearing this, his therapist, Dr. C, thought that Mr. P was putting into Dr. C parts of himself: his strength and his good vision. Mr. P experienced Dr. C as robbing him rather than himself as projecting into the therapist. Dr. C said, "You give me your strength and good sight, and then feel I robbed you." Mr. P responded, "I want to chop you up into little pieces and eat you." To this Dr. C said, "And then you could get your powers back." Mr. P replied, "That's right."

The second model of projective identification, that of Ogden, seems to apply here. In step one, Mr. P projects good parts of himself into Dr. C, possibly because he fears these good parts are in danger of attack by other aspects of himself. Probably there is some blurring of self-object representations involved in this process. In step two, Mr P sees Dr. C as having robbed him of these good parts. According to Ogden, Mr. P would have to interact directly with Dr. C, trying to make him feel and act as if he had in fact robbed Mr. P of his good parts, for this to qualify technically as a case of projective identification. Step three involves the reinternalization of the projected parts, after they have been psychologically processed by Dr. C. The psychological processing involves the chopping up of Dr. C into little pieces. The mode of the reinternalization involves a primitive incorporation.

---

*The author is indebted to Dr. Douglas Chavis for this example.

Other Ego Functions

There are other ego functions, in addition to the ones already described, that are emphasized in the literature (Bellak 1970, Bellak and Meyers 1975). The descriptions of these ego functions that follow are basically those of Bellak.

JUDGMENT

Judgment refers to the ability, first, to be aware of the likely consequences of intended or actual behavior, and second, to act in accordance with this awareness. This ego function is a complex one, clearly related to three ego functions already discussed: reality testing, impulse control and frustration tolerance, and thought processes. Isolated difficulties in judgment are common. More global difficulties are often associated with both borderline and psychotic conditions.

ADAPTIVE REGRESSION IN THE SERVICE OF THE EGO

This ego function was first described by Kris (1952), who originally used the term to characterize creativity. Adaptive regression in the service of the ego (ARISE) contains three components. The first involves the ability to suspend secondary process thinking and to allow more primitive and unconscious forms of ideation to emerge. This is the regression. The second component involves the capacity to reverse the regression readily and to return to secondary process thinking. The third component involves the capacity to use the regression for adaptive and creative ends. In addition to its clear relationship to creativity, ARISE is necessary for the pursuit of psychoanalysis. Typically obsessive-compulsive individuals display difficulty in enacting the first component, regression, and sometimes have difficulty becoming actively involved in psychoanalysis as a result. Psychotic and borderline invididuals, in contrast, have no difficulty regressing. The problem with these individuals is in the last two components: reversing the regression and using it adaptively and creatively. Because of these difficulties, borderline and psychotic individuals are generally thought to be poor candidates for psychoanalysis.

STIMULUS BARRIER

This ego function has two components. The first component, the receptive one, refers to the individual's sensitivity to and awareness of sensory stimulation, both internal and external. The second component, the expressive one, reflects the individual's ability to cope with various kinds and levels of stimulation. Individuals who are either oversensitive to stimulation or have difficulty in coping with this stimulation present special problems. Insomnia, easy distractability, and difficulty in concentrating are examples of mild difficulties regarding the stimulus barrier. More severe difficulties include disorganization and loss of control in response to overstimulation. Problems with the stimulus barrier are frequent in patients with difficulties of organic origin. Certain theoretical conceptualizations of schizophrenia (Grotstein 1977a, 1977b) have focused on defects in this ego function.

AUTONOMOUS FUNCTIONS

These ego functions have been described extensively by Hartmann (1939, 1955). The term *autonomy* basically means freedom from conflict. Primary autonomous functions are those functions with which an individual is born and that typically do not become involved in conflict. These include, among others, orientation, memory, perception, attention, intelligence, language, sensation, and motor expression. Defects in the primary autonomous functions are most often indicative of organicity. Impairments of this type are not characteristic of borderline individuals. Secondary autonomous functions are behavior patterns and traits that, although they develop out of conflict, later become free from conflict. Although these secondary autonomous functions can sometimes become reinvolved in conflict, they most often remain stable.

SYNTHESIS-INTEGRATION

Basically, this ego function represents the way the individual integrates all the other ego functions into a coherent and smoothly operating whole. It is a complex ego function, difficult to measure. The synthetic-integrative function can be described in terms of two components. The first component involves the ability to integrate potentially contradictory experiences or ideas. These include such items as self and object representations, affects, thoughts, feelings, and actions. The second component involves the ability to integrate experiences or ideas that are not contradictory. Both borderline and psychotic individuals show global impairments in this function.

CHAPTER 3

The Instinctual Drives, the Superego, and a Psychodynamic Classification of Psychopathology

The Instinctual Drives

Classical psychoanalytic theory hypothesizes the id as consisting of two instinctual drives, the libidinal drive and the aggressive drive. Together these two drives comprise the individual's psychic energy. Neither of these two drives is a concrete entity; along with the ego and the superego, they comprise hypothetical psychic structures. Psychoanalytic theory hypothesizes that these instinctual drives are active from infancy on, trying to obtain gratification and influencing behavior continuously.

There is some disagreement about how the instinctual drives develop. One modification of the theory that the infant is born with an undifferentiated pool of drive energy, which we have described in Chapter 1, hypothesizes both libidinal and aggressive drives present at birth. A second modification considers neutralized drive energy to also be present at birth. The important point is that out of the neutralized drive energy, whatever its point of origination, further psychic structure is formed, as we have described. Hartmann (Hartmann, Kris, and Lowenstein 1946), Jacobson (1964), and Brenner (1955) have all written extensively regarding this drive theory.

By age 3 the ego is well developed and differentiated. From this time on, much of human behavior and character can be described in terms of interactions among the instinctual drives, the ego, and the external world. Human behavior, before the differentiation of the ego, can be thought of as resulting from interactions among the instinctual drives, the evolving ego (or ego fragments), and the external world. By the age of 5 or 6 the superego is well developed and differentiated. Human behavior and character can now be conceptualized more complexly in terms of interactions among all three psychic structures and the external world. Before the differentiation of the superego, one can think of the evolving superego (or superego fragments) as playing a role analogous to that of the superego in this interactional process.

In understanding the dynamics of healthier individuals, including the neurotic, both libidinal and aggressive drives receive equal emphasis. In contrast, for borderline and psychotic individuals, the emphasis shifts to the aggressive drive. The borderline individual is often characterized as having an overabundance of aggressive drive. Clinically this is expressed in unmitigated anger, hostility, or rage, or by various defenses against aggression that result in feeling states such as emptiness, boredom, loneliness, and certain kinds of depression. Kernberg (1967, 1975) holds that the presence of an excessive amount of aggressive drive in the earliest (pregenital) years of life is the basic causative factor in the borderline patient. The overabundance of the aggressive drive in schizophrenia has been regularly emphasized. Outbursts of extreme aggression are frequent occurrences in acute schizophrenic states, and extreme defenses against these, such as catatonia, are well known. A number of theories point to either an excess of aggression or the inability of the individual to handle his aggression as causative in schizophrenia. Thus, Klein (1946) has hypothesized that the main defect in schizophrenia is an excess of death instinct. Bak (1954) has stated that the ego's inability to neutralize the aggressive drive constitutes the core problem in schizophrenia, and Hartmann (1953) has also related schizophrenia to the inability of the ego to neutralize aggression.

The Superego

The superego is the third hypothetical psychic structure invented to help understand the workings of the mind. The superego is thought to evolve out of neutralized drive energy from the id, and to be well formed by the age of 5 or 6 years. Like the ego, it emerges in a gradual and ongoing way. One can conceptualize an evolving superego or superego fragments as forerunners to the superego, preceding the final superego differentiation. Classical psychoanalytic theory describes the formation of the superego in relation to the resolution of the oedipus complex. Basically, the superego consists of two components: the conscience and the ego ideal. The conscience refers to moral and ethical values, what is right and what is wrong. It represents an internalization of a set of values, standards, attitudes, prohibitions, and commands, usually of parental origin. The ego ideal refers to one's aspirations, ideals, and goals; it is also heavily influenced by parental attitudes.

The superego typically disapproves of instinctual drive wishes and signals the ego to eliminate or modify them. Superego psychopathology is often apparent when the conscience is overly strict, rigid, primitive, critical, and punitive. This is often the case in various kinds of depresson. Superego pathology also readily shows itself when the self concept deviates from the ego ideal. This again is often the case in depression. Besides depression, superego pathology is clearly implicated in obsessive-compulsive states. The superego has not been emphasized in the borderline states and psychoses, possibly because preoedipal factors (those before age 3) have been given primary emphasis in understanding these conditions, whereas the superego is not thought to be well consolidated until age 5 or 6.

A Psychodynamic Classification
of Psychopathology

Throughout this book, reference is made to three large diagnostic groupings distinguished by degree of psychopathology. These groupings, in accordance with the work of Kernberg (1977, 1980a, 1980b, 1981), are the normal-neurotic, the borderline, and the psychotic. Each of these groupings is characterized by a distinct underlying structural configuration, consisting of a specific pattern of ego and superego functioning along with a specific pattern of instinctual drive organization. These configurations are stable and resist change, except via intensive psychotherapeutic intervention. The pattern of ego functioning, described in the form of a profile or inventory of ego functions, by itself is sufficient to establish a differential diagnosis among these three large groupings. "Normal" and neurotic individuals have similar ego profiles, although distinctions can be made by a close and in-depth evaluation of interpersonal relations and defensive functioning. Because these distinctions are sometimes arbitrary and subjective, the normal and neurotic are classified together to provide the "healthy" grouping in this system.

All individuals basically fall into one of these groupings. In evaluation interviews it is helpful first to classify individuals in accordance with these groupings. A "structural" diagnosis thus made is invaluable for conceptual understanding, therapeutic assessment, and prognostic appraisal, providing the framework for further discussion and evaluation. This structural diagnosis can serve as a supraordinate, or first-level diagnosis. Later a more specific and secondary diagnosis can be added, providing further descriptive information. If one desires, *DSM-III* (American Psychiatric Association 1980) diagnoses can be used as the secondary diagnoses.

The borderline patient can be conceptualized as having an ego profile characterized by four relative ego strengths and four underlying ego weaknesses. The strengths are:

1. The relative intactness of reality testing (intact in everyday interactions but vulnerable to reality distortions and brief psychotic episodes under stress)

2. The relative intactness of thought processes(secondary process in everyday interactions but vulnerable to regressions to primary process thinking under stress and in nonstructured situations)
3. The relative intactness of interpersonal relations (intact superficially but lacking in empathy and depth, and basically need fulfilling when viewed under close scrutiny)
4. The relative intactness of the adaptation to reality (intact superficially but revealing numerous difficulties in adaptation when viewed closely)

The weaknesses are:

1. The combination of poor impulse control and poor frustration tolerance
2. The proclivity to use primitive ego defenses
3. The syndrome of identity diffusion (characterized by an unstable sense of self and objects, with multiple contradictory self and object images)
4. Affective instability (characterized by intense affect, usually depressive or hostile, and by the propensity for rapid affective shifts)

The relative ego strengths differentiate the borderline from the more psychotic individual. The underlying weaknesses, correspondingly, differentiate the borderline from the more neurotic individual. Thus, the basically psychotic individual is characterized by more global defects in reality testing and thought processes, along with more obvious disturbances in interpersonal relations and the adaptation to reality. Like the borderline patient, the psychotic shows poor impulse control and poor frustration tolerance, identity diffusion, and affective instability. There is a proclivity to use primitive ego defenses, both those described as borderline and those considered narcissistic. The basically normal-neurotic individual is characterized by good reality testing, secondary process thinking, good interpersonal relations, good adaptation to reality, good impulse control and frustration tolerance, defenses typically characterized as "neurotic" or "higher level," a stable identity, and affective stability.

Kernberg (1980a, 1980b, 1981) simplifies differential diagnosis among the three major groupings by focusing on only three ego functions: reality testing, defenses, and identity diffusion. Although Kernberg would agree with the details of the ego profiles we have presented, he believes the selective focus on these three ego functions to be sufficient for differential diagnosis. In fact, he (1981) has demonstrated a high correlation between diagnoses of borderline personalities derived in this manner and such diagnoses arrived at through other approaches and psychological testing. For diagnosis alone, Kernberg's selective focus should suffice. For ascertaining as much information as possible for overall understanding and treatment planning, focus on the entire ego profile is preferable.

After the structural diagnosis is established, a secondary diagnosis can be added to provide more specificity and description. The secondary diagnoses at the normal-neurotic structural level include the "classical" neuroses and what Kernberg (1971) calls higher-level character pathology. This category contains, among others, the obsessive-compulsive neurotic, the hysterical neurotic, the depressive neurotic, some phobic neurotics, the obsessive-compulsive character, the hysterical character, the depressive character, and the masochistic character. The descriptive terms used here refer to entities described in the psychoanalytic literature, as opposed to those of *DSM-III*.

The secondary diagnoses at the borderline structural level include many of those entities that Kernberg (1971) terms lower-level character pathology. This category includes the impulse-ridden character, the infantile character, the antisocial personality, the inadequate personality, the paranoid personality, some schizoid personalities, some narcissistic personalities, some phobic neurotics, and the *DSM-III* histrionic personality. The secondary diagnoses at the psychotic structural level include mainly the classical psychoses. Thus, this category contains, among others, the schizophrenic, the manic depressive, the paranoid psychotic, and the *DSM-III* schizophreniform psychotic and major depressive.

As we will discuss in Chapter 12, it is possible to conceptualize a fourth large grouping, the narcissistic level. This grouping, again characterized by a distinct underlying structural configuration, falls in degree of psychopathology between the neurotic and the borderline level. The works of Kernberg (1970, 1974, 1975, 1976a, 1980) and Kohut (1966, 1968, 1971, 1972, 1977) on the narcissistic personality provide a basis for this additional grouping, as we will show in detail in our later discussion.

PART TWO

Diagnosis and Psychodynamics

CHAPTER 4

Early Psychoanalytic Conceptualizations

The early psychoanalytic papers discussing the borderline personality fall into one of two groups. One group viewed these patients as having a mild form of schizophrenia; the second viewed them as a distinct and separate group of patients, neither neurotic nor psychotic, but operating psychopathologically on a level between the two. Thus Zilboorg (1941) originated the term *ambulatory schizophrenia* to refer to a group of patients whom he considered to have mild schizophrenia but who could function without the need for hospitalization. Hoch and Polatin (1949) coined the term *pseudoneurotic schizophrenia* to describe patients who appeared neurotic but who under close scrutiny were revealed to be schizophrenic. The traits of pananxiety, pansexuality, and panneurosis were characteristic of this group. Analogous to this group, a group of pseudopsychopathic schizophrenic patients was described by Dunaif and Hoch (1955). Bychowsky (1953) used the term *latent psychosis* to refer to patients who had a great potential to regress and become psychotic under severe stress. The term *latent schizophrenia*, related to this conceptualization, made its way into the official nomenclature in *DSM-II* (American Psychiatric Association, 1968). The patients described in all the papers mentioned were considered within the schizophrenic group.

Other psychoanalytic papers viewed the borderline patient as distinct and separate, operating psychopathologically between the levels of neurosis and psychosis. Stern (1938) was the first to use the term *borderline* formally in this regard, describing ten criteria for making this diagnosis. Deutsch (1942) offered the term *as-if personality* to describe a group of patients who functioned as if they were normal but who under close scrutiny revealed clear pathology in their internalized object relations. Knight (1953) also used the term *borderline*, here to refer to a group of patients who, from an ego psychological point of view, displayed similarities to both neurotic and psychotic patients. Emphasizing the weakening of ego functions in these patients, he viewed this group as midline between neurosis and psychosis. Frosch (1964, 1970) introduced the term *psychotic character* to refer to patients of an intermediate range of psychopathology. Although these patients shared many ego psychological characteristics with psychotics, they differed from psychotic patients in their relative ability to preserve reality testing, their superior object relations, and their capacity for reversibility if and when they did regress. Rapaport, Gill, and Schafer (1945-1946) complemented these works by describing a group of preschizophrenic patients who, on psychological testing, revealed a predominance of primary process thinking and a generalized weakening of ego functioning compared with more neurotic patients. There are a number of other psychoanalytic papers discussing the borderline personality, but those described seem to have had the most influence on current concepts and are the most helpful in providing background for understanding.

The Ambulatory Schizophrenic (Zilboorg)

Zilboorg (1941) described a group of patients whom he considered as representing either early or mild cases of schizophrenia. These patients did not have the flagrant symptoms most often associated with advanced schizophrenia: ideas of reference, delusions, hallucinations, and flat affect. On the surface they appeared normal, often functioning in society adequately. They suffered from a number of more subtle defects, however, that Zilboorg believed indicative of schizophrenia. These patients had a tendency to be taciturn and somewhat autistic, established shallow interpersonal relationships if any, and had difficulty with long-term, goal-directed pursuits. They had overwhelming amounts of anger, yet they did not express this anger directly; rather, it was most often demonstrated in chronic tenseness and anxiety. A tendency to intellectualize and use many abstractions also helped conceal this anger. These patients often led very simple and inhibited sexual lives. They displayed a separation of sexual experiences from love, and had the tendency to masturbate without fantasy. Often there was the propensity to overindulge in alcohol consumption. To the observer these patients seemed like "difficult people" or "problem children" rather than schizophrenics.

To this group of individuals Zilboorg assigned the name *ambulatory schizophrenics*. They were ambulatory, as evidenced by their ability to participate in life in a manner that seemed somewhat normal. Zilboorg believed that, although they did not exhibit the flagrant symptoms of schizophrenia, this group suffered from the basic underlying schizophrenic process. If we take an ego psychological approach to Zilboorg's patients (an approach to be elaborated on later), we can characterize them as demonstrating difficulties with thought processes, interpersonal relations, adaptation to reality, impulse control and frustration tolerance, and affective stability. Although generally more psychopathological than the typical borderline patient described today, a number of these patients might fulfill the criteria for some of the modern classifications of borderline personality.

The Pseudoneurotic Schizophrenic
(Hoch and Polatin)

Hoch and Polatin (1949) described a group of patients who showed a rather definite clinical syndrome of pananxiety, panneurosis, and pansexuality. Although these individuals appeared highly neurotic, close scrutiny revealed schizophrenia. Often these patients had started psychoanalytic treatment before the severe nature of their underlying psychopathology was known. To this syndrome Hoch and Polatin assigned the name *pseudoneurotic schizophrenia*.

These patients were characterized by an all-pervasive anxiety, an anxiety virtually always manifest and not bound or decreased by specific symptoms. These patients were notable for the abundance of neurotic symptoms present at the same time, including hysteric, vegetative, phobic, obsessive-compulsive, and depressive symptoms. The symptoms would characteristically shift rapidly but would almost always be present. In addition, these patients usually showed a tendency for sexual preoccupations based in all levels of libidinal development, providing a kind of "polymorphous perverse" and sexually chaotic picture. These patterns gave rise to the descriptive terms *pananxiety*, *panneurosis*, and *pansexuality*. In addition, the pseudoneurotic was characterized by a lack of modulation and flexibility in emotional display, an emotional coldness, and yet a hypersensitivity to emotional situations. A kind of overt hatred, more open and less discriminating than in the typical neurotic, was often seen.

Hoch and Polatin, like Zilboorg, believed that these patients demonstrated the Bleulerian pathognomonic signs of schizophrenia. They noted, however, that these pathognomonic signs were often shown in subtle rather than global ways. The basic autistic life approach, although present, was not always apparent. Ambivalence was seen in greater quantities than in the neurotic but was often difficult to evaluate. Affect was characterized by a subtle lack of modulation and flexibility. Gross thought disorders were absent, although a number of the more subtle signs, such as condensations and displacements, omnipotent attitudes, and thought magic, were present. Psychological testing sometimes revealed a thinking disorder but sometimes did not. In essence, at times it was not objectively demonstrable whether these highly anxious and overtly neurotic-appearing patients actually showed the underlying signs of schizophrenia. Hoch and Polatin viewed these patients as schizophrenic, but there appear to be patients having symptoms of pananxiety, panneurosis, and pansexuality who reveal an ego psychological pattern characteristic of borderline psychopathology rather than schizophrenia.

The Latent Psychotic (Bychowsky)

Bychowsky (1953) described a group of patients who did not appear psychotic on the surface yet had the potential to regress and become psychotic under stress. To this group of individuals he gave the name *latent psychotics*. Bychowsky identified five categories of individuals who fit into this group:

1. Individuals with character (or personality) disorders who "burst" into psychoses under stress
2. Individuals functioning as psychoneurotics who likewise "burst" into psychoses under stress
3. Socially deviant individuals, such as addicts, delinquents, and individuals with perversions, who had an underlying ego structure vulnerable to psychotic regression
4. Individuals with "arrested" psychoses who later would reveal their psychotic potential
5. Individuals who became psychotic under the stress of psychoanalysis or dynamically oriented psychotherapy.

Bychowsky noted a number of features characteristic of this group of patients. There was a tendency, particularly in psychoanalysis, for "increased communication between the mental systems," such that primary process prevailed too often in the patient's productions. There was a vulnerability to regression and overreaction to frustrations; a primitive megalomania; the use of primitive defenses, magical thinking, and ideas of reference; evidence of poor development of ego boundaries; and a primitive, unsublimated, and nonneutralized aggression. Bychowsky viewed these patients as basically psychotic, often using psychological testing to help arrive at this diagnosis. From an ego psychological point of view, however, with a focus on problems in reality testing, thought processes, impulse control and frustration tolerance, defenses employed, and affective stability, some of these patients may well be seen to fit into the borderline group.

The Borderline Group (Stern)

Stern (1938) was the first to use the term *borderline*. He differed from the previous three authors in that he viewed the borderline patient not as basically psychotic but, rather, as having a kind of stable psychopathology, somewhere between neurosis and psychosis in severity. In this conceptualization he predated Kernberg by a number of years. Like others, Stern found these patients to be highly resistant to psychoanalysis. He characterized the borderline personality by ten features:

1. *Narcissism.* Although Stern did not define this term, he spoke of narcissism in relation to early developmental failures in parenting. He described very disturbed, cruel, detached, and depriving mothers.
2. *Psychic bleeding.* Stern used this term to refer to the patient's paralysis, immobility, and lethargy in response to crises.
3. *Inordinate hypersensitivity.* This term referred to the patient's oversensitivity and vulnerability to slights, criticisms, and rejections.
4. *Psychic rigidity.* This term referred not only to the patient's stiff posture, but also to a generalized rigidity and inflexibility in defensive patterns.
5. *Negative therapeutic reaction.* Stern used this term to refer to the patient's negative reaction, often demonstrated in anger, discouragement, or a worsening of symptoms, to the therapist's interventions. This response was often related to the patient's feeling criticized, hurt, or rejected by the therapist's comments. At other times an interpretation would produce anxiety and the patient's negative response would allow him or her to avoid this anxiety.
6. *Feelings of inferiority.* Stern characterized the borderline patient as having pervasive feelings of inferiority, feelings

that were sometimes ego syntonic. The patient often used these feelings to avoid constructive thinking or action.

7. *Masochism.* This term referred to the tendency of the patient to indulge in self-pity and to present himself as suffering, helpless, and injured. Depression often accompanied these masochistic feelings.

8. *Somatic insecurity or anxiety.* Stern believed that the borderline individual demonstrated a deep underlying insecurity going back to earliest childhood. Self-assurance and self-confidence were consistently absent.

9. *The use of projective mechanisms.* The borderline individual showed a strong tendency to use projective mechanisms.

10. *Difficulties in reality testing.* Stern described problems in this area as they occurred in the transference. The difficulties were not a global inability to distinguish internal from external stimuli but, rather, a more subtle and common distortion of reality based on the infantile past. Basically, the analyst was viewed and treated as an omnipotent, omniscient figure.

Stern's borderline patients seem like healthier individuals than those thus far described. In some ways these patients are not unlike Kohut's narcissistic personalities (1966, 1968, 1971, 1972, 1977). Depending on what diagnostic system one uses, some of these patients may still fit into the borderline category. The relationship of Kohut's narcissistic personality to the borderline personality will be explored later, in Chapter 12.

The As-If Personality (Deutsch)

Deutsch (1942) described a group of patients who first appeared normal, but who nevertheless suffered from marked emotional impoverishment and pathology of their internalized object relations. As one observed these patients further, something intangible and indefinable stood out that made one invariably ask what was wrong. Their entire relationship to life seemed lacking in genuineness. Their interpersonal relationships seemed mature, yet there was something strange and stilted about them. Under closer observation these relationships turned out to be devoid of any warmth, concern, or empathy. These people acted as if they were normal and complete, yet beneath this façade they were troubled. To these individuals Deutsch assigned the name *as-if* personalities.

These individuals, in an attempt to act normal, had a tendency to adopt the qualities of whomever they had contact with. These qualities could change rapidly as the individual came under the influence of different people. Analogous shifts occurred in these people's ideals, convictions, and aspirations. These shifts were understood by Deutsch to be attempts to overcome what actually was an inner emptiness. These individuals were further characterized by their suggestibility, their marked passivity, and their feelings of depersonalization and derealization. All these individuals showed a deep disturbance in their sublimatory and synthetic functions, failing to synthesize their various infantile identifications into integrated identities.

Deutsch noted that her patients tested reality well and thus could not be considered psychotic, yet they clearly seemed sicker than the usual neurotic. Like Stern, Deutsch viewed these individuals as having a kind of stable psychopathology, somewhere between neurosis and psychosis in severity. She viewed the cause of the disturbances to be impaired object relations. Both her descriptions and her view of the psychopathology are echoed in Kernberg's later concept of identity diffusion. Her work can thus be seen as a forerunner of Kernberg's in this regard. From an ego psychological point of view, many of Deutsch's patients would now fit within the borderline group.

The Borderline State (Knight)

Knight (1953) followed Stern in actually using the term *borderline*. He focused on patients who used both neurotic and psychotic mechanisms and had not yet "broken with reality," but who demonstrated sufficient maladjustment and ominous clinical signs to preclude the diagnosis of psychoneurosis. Knight strongly emphasized an ego psychological approach in the evaluation of these patients. His patients demonstrated superficial adaptation to the environment, a superficial maintenance of interpersonal relations, and reality testing that also appeared intact on the surface. Autonomous ego functions such as memory, calculating ability, and certain habitual performances were unimpaired. There were weaknesses, however, in secondary process thinking, integration, realistic planning, concept formation, judgment, and defenses against primitive unconscious impulses. Also, in a pattern similar to that described by Hoch and Polatin, the clinical picture was dominated by a variety of neurotic symptoms.

Knight spoke of careful psychiatric interviewing and psychological testing as ways of providing more precise evaluation of the various disturbances in these patients. Through these techniques, Knight developed long lists of macroscopic and microscopic evidence of ego weakness. He cited as macroscopic evidence a lack of concern over the predicament, an absence of observable precipitating stress, a viewing of symptoms as ego syntonic or externally precipitated, a lack of achievement over time, unrealistic planning, the relating of bizarre dreams, and insufficient contrasts between dreams and waking life. Microscopic evidence included impaired integration of ideas, impaired concept formation, impaired judgment, occasional blocking, peculiarities of word usage, obliviousness to obvious implications, contaminations of idioms, occasional inappropriate affect, suspicion-laden questions and behavior, and lack of recognition of or embarrassment over peculiarities of speech.

Knight's conception of the borderline state existing somewhere between neurosis and psychosis is still accepted today. The overwhelming emphasis on a wide variety of ego impairments, however, makes one suspect that at least some of his patients might now be classified as demonstrating mild schizophrenia. Others, however, might fit into contemporary descriptions of the borderline group.

The Psychotic Character (Frosch)

Frosch (1964, 1970) described a group of patients whom he considered to be neither neurotic nor psychotic but to represent a level of psychopathology intermediate between these two. Frosch believed that these patients formed a unified group having specific and stable psychopathology. Barring certain features, these people would be psychotic, and in fact they could regress to psychoses at times of stress. What distinguished these patients from the psychotic was their relative ability to preserve reality testing, their superior object relations, their capacity for rapid reversibility when regressions did occur, and the presence of a reality-syntonic adaptation. However these patients showed many disturbances characteristic of psychosis as well. To this group of patients Frosch assigned the name *psychotic character*.

Much of Frosch's article is concerned with a description of reality. In a similar but somewhat different focus from Bellak (1958) and Bellak and Meyers (1975), Frosch divided reality into three components: the relationship with reality, the feeling of reality, and the capacity to test reality. The relationship with reality, somewhat analogous to Bellak's adaptation to reality, involves the appropriateness of the individual's reactions to internal and external events. The feeling of reality is virtually identical to Bellak's sense of reality. The capacity to test reality is likewise synonymous with Bellak's reality testing. According to Frosch, in the psychotic all three components of reality are deficient. In contrast, the psychotic character has obvious disturbances in the relationship with reality and the feeling of reality yet maintains a relative capacity to test reality. Some vulnerability in reality testing is demonstrated by the sensitivity of this ego function to regression at times of stress. At these times, miniature psychotic episodes can occur, but because of the ego's capacity to reverse regressions rapidly, these episodes are always brief.

In his concept of the relationship to reality, Frosch includes both internal and external reality. Hallucinations, illusions, and self-object fusion are considered defects in this area. The point is that the psychotic character can experience these perceptual distortions while his intact reality testing enables him to tell that they are, in fact, distortions. This is analogous to an individual's experiencing feelings of depersonalization, derealization, *déjà vu*, and the like while his intact reality testing helps him to realize that they are only feelings. The intactness of the reality testing actually at times helps limit or decrease the problems in the relationship with reality and the feeling of reality. Frosch described a wide range of degrees of vulnerability to regression in reality testing. Some of his patients never regressed in reality testing; others, more typical, seemed to be continually going through a series of regressions followed by reversals.

Frosch emphasized that his patients represented a specific and stable intermediate level of psychopathology, neither neurotic nor psychotic. His emphasis here was more than that of his predecessors—Stern, Deutsch, and Knight—and clearly previewed Kernberg's concept. Like Knight, Frosch took a definite ego psychological approach to differentiate his patients from the typical psychotic individual. Many of Frosch's patients would fit into the borderline group as described today.

CHAPTER 5

Borderline Personality Organization (Kernberg)

This chapter will present Kernberg's ideas and concepts in a simplified yet comprehensive manner. At times there will be some modifications, clarifications, and additions to Kernberg's original writings. However, Kernberg's basic ideas and concepts are unaltered; thus, this chapter provides a useful presentation of Kernberg's conceptualization of the borderline personality. Parts of this chapter are related to several previous publications on the topic (Goldstein 1982, 1983, 1985b).

The Borderline Personality as an Underlying Structural Configuration

Kernberg pictures the borderline as a specific, stable pathological personality organization, characterized by a specific kind of underlying structural configuration. This structural configuration includes a specific kind of ego and superego functioning and a specific pattern of instinctual drive organization. This configuration is stable and resistant to change except via intensive psychotherapeutic intervention. According to this approach, the diagnosis of borderline personality should be made only in the presence of the underlying borderline structural configuration. Symptoms and personality traits are interpreted in accordance with the structural configuration and are never diagnostic by themselves.

According to Kernberg, there are three levels of psychic functioning, with corresponding distinct structural configurations: the neurotic, the borderline, and the psychotic. Diagnostically, all patients can be classified into one of these groups. As noted, in evaluation interviews it is helpful first to classify individuals in accordance with these structural configurations and thus to establish a supraordinate diagnosis. It is important to emphasize that the borderline level of functioning is a supraordinate, or first-level, diagnosis, under which a number of more specific diagnoses fall. This diagnostic approach is in marked contrast to a more descriptive approach also prevalent today. This latter approach, to be detailed later, views the borderline as one of a number of distinct personality disorders, as opposed to a supraordinate diagnosis.

Correlation with Other Approaches

It is useful to contrast Kernberg's approach—structural diagnosis—with the descriptive approach to the borderline personality. The latter approach is subscribed to by those psychiatrists, often researchers, who are most interested in establishing a description of the borderline personality that is simple, reliable, and valid. The primary focus here is on symptoms and traits, particularly those that most clearly differentiate the borderline from other groups of patients. Literature reviews, research designs, and statistical methods are employed to try to identify those traits and symptoms. Typically, long checklists are utilized to make this differentiation. The work of Perry and Klerman (1978, 1980), Gunderson (1977), and Gunderson and Kolb (1978) is representative of this group. *DSM-III* also falls into this category.

In theory, Kernberg's structural approach is much different from the descriptive approach. In actual diagnostic practice, however, there may be little difference between the two. Kernberg,(Kernberg, Goldstein, Carr, et al., 1981) has demonstrated a high correlation between the results of his method of diagnosis and that of Gunderson. There would likely also be a high correlation between the results of Kernberg's method and the approach in *DSM-III*. Kernberg (1980b) believes that, although his approach to the borderline personality is quite different from that of *DSM-III*, the two approaches are compatible and can complement each other.

Characteristics of the Borderline Structural Configuration

Returning to the borderline as a level of psychic functioning with an underlying structural configuration, we will now take a closer look at that configuration. The borderline is a specific, stable pathological personality organization. It is specific in that it is characterized by a specific structural configuration, stable in that this structural configuration is very resistant to change except via major psychotherapeutic intervention, and pathological in that marked underlying weaknesses characterize the structural configuration. Although the structural configuration includes a specific kind of ego and superego functioning, as well as a specific pattern of instinctual drive organization, the emphasis in Kernberg's work is predominantly on the ego.

THE EGO IN THE BORDERLINE PERSONALITY

In characterizing the ego in the borderline personality, Kernberg focuses on:

1. Reality testing
2. Nonspecific manifestations of ego weakness

    a. Lack of anxiety tolerance
    b. Lack of impulse control
    c. Lack of sublimatory channels
 3. Shifts toward primary process thinking
 4. Specific defensive operations
 5. Pathological internalized object relations, characterized by
    identity diffusion

Basically, Kernberg focuses on the six ego functions elaborated
on in Chapter 2.

Reality Testing

Reality testing in day-to-day functioning is basically intact in the
borderline patient. In his recent writings, Kernberg (1980a,
1981) focuses on this intactness of reality testing as a main
factor in the differential diagnoses between the borderline and
the psychotic structural configurations. Despite this intactness,
under stress and in very close interpersonal situations, there is
a tendency for this ego function to regress. A regression under
stress can lead to brief psychotic episodes. Some think that a
distinction can be drawn between the borderline patient and
the schizophrenic by the nature of the symptoms during these
psychotic episodes. Kernberg holds, however, that this distinction is difficult to make, and that the symptomatology of the
borderline patient during these psychotic episodes is often
indistinguishable from that of the true psychotic. What distinguishes these episodes is their brevity, their reversibility, and
their relationship to clear-cut precipitating events. Kernberg
particularly notes that these episodes are likely to occur with
the use of drugs or alcohol or in relation to a transference
regression during intense psychotherapy. Any obvious stress
and any intense interpersonal interaction, however, can trigger
the regression. Kernberg does not state exactly how brief or
transient these episodes are, but it is safe to assume that they
can be as brief as a few minutes and certainly no longer than a
day or two. Some borderline patients never evidence such
episodes. Thus, these transient psychotic episodes under stress

are seen as allowable but certainly not mandatory in making the diagnosis of borderline.

Nonspecific Ego Weakness

Kernberg refers to the lack of anxiety (or frustration) tolerance, the lack of impulse control, and lack of developed sublimatory channels as nonspecific aspects of ego weakness in the borderline patient. The first two of these have been described in detail in Chapter 2. These difficulties most frequently present themselves clinically in the borderline in the tendency toward states of disruptive anger, the tendency to use drugs or alcohol to avoid frustration and obtain temporary gratification, and the tendency to flee the work or interpersonal situation under stress.

Kernberg lists the lack of developed sublimatory channels as a third nonspecific ego weakness, especially noting a lack of creative enjoyment and creative achievement in the borderline individual. The patient typically does not use sublimation or other higher-level defenses. Although the lack of developed sublimatory channels certainly seems characteristic of the borderline individual, it is somewhat unclear why Kernberg views this trait as a nonspecific ego weakness, instead of considering it when he discusses defensive functioning.

Shifts Toward Primary Process Thinking

Thought processes, in day-to-day functioning and in structured situations, are predominantly secondary process. Under acute stress and in unstructured situations (such as projective psychological testing), however, primary process often emerges. Kernberg believes that projective psychological evaluation will invariably reveal primary process thinking in borderline patients, a position substantiated in a research project in which psychological tests were administered to a number of borderline patients (Kernberg, Goldstein, Carr, et al. 1981). The pattern of secondary process on the WAIS and primary process on the Rorschach was very clear. Nevertheless, personal experience here has not been so conclusive, particularly in regard to consistent use of primary process on the Rorschach. One reason for this difference may be the variation in the way individuals use psychological tests to make diagnoses. Certainly, however, the tendency for the borderline patient to reveal primary process thinking on the Rorschach but not the WAIS must be noted.

Specific Defensive Operations

Central in Kernberg's conceptualization of the borderline patient is the role of certain specific primitive defenses in these individuals. Kernberg describes six primitive defenses that he feels are both characteristic of and pathognomonic for the borderline state. These include splitting, primitive idealization, early forms of projection and projective identification, denial, omnipotence, and devaluation. Of these defenses Kernberg considers splitting to be of central importance, analogous to repression in the neurotic. Kernberg's conceptual understanding of the borderline personality, as will be elaborated on later, centers on the role of splitting in early development. In essence, Kernberg describes early development as normally characterized by the use of splitting and related primitive mechanisms. As part of normal development, these primitive mechanisms are replaced by higher-level mechanisms centering on repression. In the borderline individual this change does not occur, and the use of splitting and related primitive mechanisms persists.

Kernberg clearly states that the use of these primitive defenses is crucial for both the diagnosis and the conceptual understanding of the borderline personality. He does not indicate either the frequency with which such defenses are used in adult life, however, or the extent to which the use of these defenses precludes the additional use of higher-level defenses. The typical borderline individual, in usual day-to-day functioning, does not use predominantly borderline defenses, but, rather, a combination of neurotic, immature, and borderline defenses. Under stress the borderline displays the tendency to use borderline and, occasionally, narcissistic defenses. The exact combination of defenses used in day-to-day functioning varies enormously from individual to individual, but the tendency to use the borderline defenses under stress is what is most characteristic of the defensive pattern of this group of patients. Hence, the borderline personality uses primitive defenses more than the neurotic in day-to-day functioning, relying on them to a greater extent under stress. Details about Kernberg's six borderline defenses have already been discussed in Chapter 2.

Other writers are not as specific as Kernberg as to the exact primitive defenses used by the borderline patient. Agreement is more universal about the tendency of the borderline patient to use some primitive defenses, including those emphasized by Kernberg.

Pathological Internalized Object Relations

Kernberg uses Erikson's term *identity diffusion* (1956) to describe the pathological internalized object relations of the borderline patient. Other terms frequently used to describe this problem include the lack of an integrated self concept, the lack of a sense of self, the lack of a real self, the lack of a stable identity, and the lack of a coherent sense of self. The terms *as-if personality* (Deutsch 1942) and *false self* (Winnicott 1965) are also relevant here. In Mahler's terms (Mahler, Pine, and Bergman 1975) the individual has not attained libidinal object constancy.

THE SUPEREGO IN THE BORDERLINE PERSONALITY

As noted, Kernberg's approach to borderline structural psychopathology centers on the ego. The essential strengths and weaknesses that most easily differentiate the borderline from the neurotic and the psychotic reside in the ego. Kernberg notes that superego characteristics are less helpful in the differential diagnosis of the borderline patient and that they show marked variation from one individual to another. Nevertheless, a lack of superego integration, corresponding to the lack of ego integration, is typical in these individuals. The ego ideal is often overidealized, based on all good self and object images. The conscience often includes sadistic components based on all bad images and is easily externalized. There is often the inability to experience true guilt, along with difficulties in experiencing true concern. Kernberg emphasizes the importance of some overall integration of the superego in attaining a good prognosis with long-term intensive psychotherapy.

THE ID IN THE BORDERLINE PERSONALITY

Kernberg does not focus extensively on id characteristics, particularly when considering the differential diagnosis of the borderline personality. However, the prevalence of pregenital aggression as a developmental and causative factor is emphasized. A condensation of pregenital and genital conflicts is noted, with a premature development of oedipal conflicts in the second or third year of life. Various kinds of behavioral patterns emerge from these phenomena. These patterns often seem chaotic initially, because they represent combinations of various underlying conflicts. On the surface there can be pansexuality and chaos; underneath, as noted, there is a combination of genital and pregenital conflicts, under the influence of excessive aggression.

SUMMARY OF THE BORDERLINE PERSONALITY AS A STRUCTURAL CONFIGURATION

The borderline is viewed as a specific, stable pathological personality organization, having its own specific underlying structural configuration. The ego is characterized by reality testing that is basically intact but vulnerable to regressions, including acute, transient, reversible psychotic episodes under stress. The nonspecific ego weaknesses of poor anxiety (or frustration) tolerance, poor impulse control, and the lack of developed sublimatory channels are invariably present.

Thought processes, although predominantly secondary process on the surface and in day-to-day functioning, are vulnerable to shifts to primary process under stress or in unstructured situations. There is a tendency to use primitive ego defenses, particularly under stress, including splitting, primitive idealization, early forms of projection and projective identification, denial, omnipotence, and devaluation. There also is a syndrome of identity diffusion, characterized by the lack of a stable and integrated self concept, along with a corresponding lack of a stable and integrated concept of others. The superego is characterized by a lack of integration, a conscience that often includes sadistic (all bad) components that are easily externalized, and an ego ideal that is often overidealized, based on all good self and object images. The instinctual drives are characterized by an overabundance of pregenital aggression leading to a condensation of pregenital and genital conflicts and resultant chaotic behavior patterns.

Diagnosis of the Borderline Personality

The definitive diagnosis of borderline personality should be made only on the basis of the structural picture. It is best made only after an in-depth examination of the patient, based on both interviews and history. To aid in structural diagnosis, Kernberg (1977, 1981) has developed what he terms the *structural interview*. This interview, by a series of clarifications, confrontations, and interpretations, focuses in depth on three ego characteristics: reality testing, defensive functioning, and identity diffusion. Kernberg believes that a differential diagnosis among borderline, neurotic, and psychotic structural configurations can be made by the selective focusing on these three characteristics. To maximize the efficiency of this approach, a series of structural interviews would be most helpful.

Descriptive Aspects

Although a definitive diagnosis should be made only on the basis of the structural picture, certain symptoms or personality constellations outlined by Kernberg are suggestive of the borderline personality in that a large number of patients with these presentations, under close scrutiny, will turn out to be in the borderline group. Kernberg emphasizes that these symptoms and personality constellations are only suggestive; they certainly can also occur in someone with a basically neurotic structural configuration.

With this caveat in mind, we will present a simplified summary of those symptoms Kernberg considers suggestive:

1. Excessive, chronic, free-floating anxiety, particularly when combined with other symptoms
2. Multiple neurotic symptoms evidenced simultaneously
3. Any neurotic symptom that appears quite bizarre or very disabling
4. Multiple perverse trends

These symptoms are reminiscent of those described by Hoch and Polatin (1949). Kernberg elaborates the following discrete symptom complexes thought to be suggestive of the borderline state:

1. Multiple phobias, especially those imposing severe restrictions on the patient's daily life, those related to the patient's body or appearance, and those involving transitional elements toward obsessive neurosis (such as the fear of dirt)
2. Obsessive-compulsive symptoms that either have acquired secondary ego syntonicity about which the patient continually rationalizes, or are of a paranoid or hypochondriacal nature
3. Dissociative reactions, especially hysterical "twilight states" and fugues, and amnesia accompanied by disturbances of consciousness
4. Expressive hypochondriasis
5. Paranoid and hypochondriacal trends when accompanied by any other symptomatic neuroses

Kernberg also refers to two rather specific constellations including multiple perverse trends. One consists of a manifest sexual behavior that is completely inhibited, accompanied by conscious fantasies, often with masturbation, involving multiple perverse trends. These fantasies are necessary for sexual gratification. The second constellation consists of manifest sexual behavior that includes multiple perverse trends.

As noted, Kernberg also states that certain personality types often are indicative of the borderline personality. In essence, many schizoid personalities, many hypomanic personalities, and most paranoid personalities would fit into this group. Most impulse-ridden characters, most infantile characters, many narcissistic personalities, and almost all antisocial personalities would fit here also. Many histrionic personalities described in *DSM-III*, although certainly not the classically defined hysterical personalities, could also be included in this group. Higher-level character traits that typically are lacking in the borderline patient include empathy, humor, creativity, warmth, dedication, tactfulness, concern, understanding, interpersonal depth, and true guilt.

Developmental Theory

A sophisticated object relations theory presented in Kernberg's second book (1976a) underlies his work. The infant is thought to organize his experiences according to affect states, initially all good and all bad. At first self and object representations are fused, and linked with either a positive (all good) or negative (all bad) affect. By the end of the first year, self representations have been differentiated from object representations. Now self and object representations are separately linked to positive (all good) and negative (all bad) affects, so that there are discrete units of self representations, object representations, and affect states. These discrete units gradually evolve into more complex psychic structures.

Mahler (Mahler, Pine, and Bergman 1975) provides a widely accepted developmental model, which can be used to explain Kernberg's object relations model. Although the developmental model of Mahler has an emphasis somewhat different from that of Kernberg's, the two are clearly compatible. In recent writings, Kernberg (1980a) himself seems disposed to use Mahler's model, even modifying his original time-table in accordance with her work. Here Mahler's model will be invoked to help understand Kernberg's formulations.

EARLY OBJECT RELATIONS

Mahler postulates that during the early months of life, the child goes through an autistic phase (of approximately 1 month's duration) during which he is oblivious to anything except himself, followed by a symbiotic phase (lasting until 5 to 10 months of age) in which he views his mother (or primary love object) as an extension of himself. This is followed by a separation–individuation phase (lasting until age 2 or 3 years) in which the child gradually differentiates and separates himself from his mother and begins to establish his identity as a person in his own right. It is only at the completion of this stage that the child has attained libidinal object constancy (a concept we will define later). In her descriptions of all events of the autistic, symbiotic, and separation–individuation phases, Mahler is speaking of intrapsychic phenomena.

Around the time of the transition from the symbiotic to the separation–individuation phase, the child begins to be able to distinguish himself intrapsychically from his mother. This phenomenon is most obvious clinically when the child develops stranger anxiety, as has been eloquently described by Spitz (1965). This momentous accomplishment, the ability of the child to distinguish himself from his mother, is synonymous with the child's acquiring the capacity to test reality and corresponds to Federn's concept of establishing ego boundaries (1952) and to Kernberg's concept of being able to differentiate self images from object images (1967, 1975).

THE CORE DEVELOPMENTAL DEFECT IN THE PSYCHOTIC

According to Kernberg, a failure in this developmental task— the ability to differentiate self images from object images, to establish ego boundaries, to test reality, and to separate oneself intrapsychically from one's mother—is the core developmental defect in the psychotic individual. The borderline individual basically has been able to accomplish this developmental task; in his case the main developmental problem comes later. However, this mastery usually remains far from total. This would explain the ease with which reality testing in the borderline individual can break down under stress or in close interpersonal relationships.

THE CORE DEVELOPMENTAL DEFECT IN THE BORDERLINE INDIVIDUAL

According to Kernberg, even before the child has accomplished the developmental task of self-object differentiation, from early infancy on, she organizes her experiences according to whether they are perceived as positive or negative. She groups experiences into two categories, good and bad. Thus, she sees her mother as either all good or all bad. She is the good mother whenever she gratifies the infant's needs, soothes her, and is ever present; she is the bad mother whenever she frustrates the infant or is absent. Even at age 1 1/2, when the child has developed object permanency (Piaget's concept [1954] of a stable visual representation of the mother whether she is present or absent), she still views the mother as either a good mother or a bad mother. When the mother frustrates the infant, or leaves, the child remembers her very well visually, yet the child's emotional feelings toward the mother change, and she is perceived as nongratifying and bad.

This tendency to perceive objects as all good or all bad, earlier described by Klein (1946) and termed splitting, is used by the child as a primary organizing principle until somewhere between the ages of 2 and 3. In a gradual process described eloquently by McDevitt (1975), the child gives up splitting and attains libidinal object constancy. Libidinal object constancy is defined as the ability of the child to maintain an emotional image of the mother as being basically good but as having both good and bad qualities, an emotional image that changes little under frustration or during absence. As already stated, this developmental task is not completed until age 2 or 3.

The attainment of libidinal object constancy is the developmental task that is lacking in the borderline patient. Although Kernberg does not use the term *libidinal object constancy*, he states that the borderline individual has failed in the task of "the integration of self and object images built up under the influence of libidinal drive derivatives with their corresponding self and object images built up under the influence of aggressive drive derivatives" (1967, p 664). This is equivalent to saying that the borderline individual has not attained libidinal object constancy and still uses splitting as a primary organizing principle.

The tendency of the borderline individual to employ splitting is not an all-or-none phenomenon. Just as the psychotic does not always test reality poorly, the borderline individual does not always split. It is more that such persons had some difficulty, varying from individual to individual, in completing the developmental task of attaining libidinal object constancy. Depending on the individual, this problem can show itself, at one extreme, as an ever-present defect in this area or, at the other extreme, as a defect that occurs only defensively under stress. Although Kernberg emphasizes the defensive nature of splitting, it seems reasonable to conclude that the vast majority of borderline patients will fall somewhere between these two extremes. Kernberg is not entirely clear in describing how splitting, once a developmental defect, later becomes used as a defense (Meissner 1978b).

Hartmann (1955) has described how, in normal development, libidinal (good) and aggressive (bad) energies are neutralized and then used for ego and superego formation. Kernberg describes how, because of the tendency to split, this neutralization cannot take place sufficiently in the borderline personality. This inability interferes not only with ego and superego integration, but also with normal modulation and differentiation of affects and with the attainment of an integrated self concept and a stable identity.

The presence of an excessive amount of aggressive drive in the earliest (pregenital) years of life, according to Kernberg, is the basic causative factor in the borderline condition. This excessive amount of aggressive drive interferes with the unfolding of the separation–individuation process in such a way that splitting is reinforced and libidinal object constancy is never truly attained. According to Kernberg, this excessive aggressive drive is either due to congenital factors or secondary to early frustrations. Although Kernberg leaves unclear the relative importance of these congenital and environmental factors, some theorists (Meissner 1978b) believe that his primary emphasis is on constitutional factors.

DEVELOPMENTAL DISTINCTIONS AMONG THE PSYCHOTIC, THE BORDERLINE, AND THE NEUROTIC STATES

The core developmental defect in the psychotic, originating in the first year of life, is the inability to differentiate self images from object images. The most obvious manifestation of this defect is the lack of reality testing. In contrast, the core developmental defect in the borderline individual, originating between the first and third years of life, is the inability to attain libidinal object constancy. The most obvious manifestation of this is the tendency to split. Using the theories of Kernberg, we can distinguish the psychotic, borderline, and neurotic states developmentally as follows. The psychotic fails in the differentiation of self from object images, does not attain libidinal object constancy, displays identity diffusion, and has a poorly formed ego. The borderline individual basically is able to differentiate self from object images but has not attained libidinal object constancy. He has a relatively weak ego and displays identity diffusion. The neurotic has no difficulty in self-object differentiation, has attained libidinal object constancy, and has a stable ego and an integrated self concept. Developmentally, the neurotic's problems originate after age 3 and are related to interpersonal relationships involving herself and significant others.

CHAPTER 6

An Ego Psychological Diagnostic
Approach to the Borderline Personality

This chapter will outline an ego psychological diagnostic approach to the borderline personality, based primarily on the work of Kernberg, with modifications, and including some additional aspects of the borderline constellation not stressed by him. The diagnostic approach outlined here attempts to provide an integrative summary of Kernberg's work and other current dynamic concepts regarding the borderline personality. Although this approach is clearly dynamically based, it is presented in such a way that it can be used easily by those more interested in description than in dynamics. Additionally, this approach can be studied using the research-oriented methods described in the next chapter, in an effort to obtain reliability and validity. This chapter is related to several previously published papers (Goldstein 1981b, 1982, 1983, 1985b).

In accordance with Kernberg, the borderline personality is considered a specific, stable, pathological personality organization, characterized by a specific kind of underlying structural configuration. Although the structural configuration includes a specific kind of ego and superego functioning, as well as a specific pattern of instinctual drive organization, the focus for diagnostic purposes will be largely on the ego.

Relying on the model of Beres (1956) and Bellak (1958), the ego of the borderline individual will be viewed according to its various ego functions. The ego is described as having a particular structure, consisting of a specific pattern of relative ego strengths and underlying ego weaknesses. The relative ego strengths are as follows:

1. The relative intactness of reality testing
2. The relative intactness of thought processes
3. The relative intactness of interpersonal relations
4. The relative intactness of the adaptation to reality

These four strengths are only relative; they easily break down to various degrees in various situations, to be described later. Because these four relative strengths stand out superficially, they enable the borderline individual to present a fairly "normal" appearance. These relative strengths, particularly the first two, most clearly differentiate the borderline from the more psychotic individual.

The underlying ego weaknesses are as follows:

1. The combination of poor impulse control and poor frustration tolerance
2. The proclivity to use primitive ego defenses
3. The syndrome of identity diffusion
4. Affective instability

In contrast to the strengths, these weaknesses become apparent only with a more in-depth understanding of the individual. Except during regressed states, a detailed history or a relationship with the individual over time is usually needed for these weaknesses to emerge clearly. Kernberg's structural interview (1977, 1981) is also helpful in learning about these weaknesses. Because these weaknesses are not detectable superficially, they do not detract from the borderline's surface appearance of normality. These underlying weaknesses, however, most clearly differentiate the borderline from the more neurotic individual.

The Relative Ego Strengths

REALITY TESTING

Reality testing is basically intact, except under stress, and in close interpersonal situations. A regression under stress can lead to brief psychotic episodes, described earlier.

THOUGHT PROCESSES

Thought processes are predominantly secondary process. Under acute stress and in unstructured situations (such as projective psychological testing), however, primary process often emerges. Although there is the tendency to find a psychological test pattern of secondary process on the WAIS and primary process on the Rorschach, there is much disagreement as to how frequently this test pattern actually occurs in borderline patients. Such findings are presumptive evidence for the diagnosis of borderline, but they are clearly not necessary for this diagnosis.

INTERPERSONAL RELATIONS

Interpersonal relations are often intact superficially. On the surface the borderline seems to "relate" to others, can have many acquaintances, and occasionally can even maintain long-term relationships. Under close scrutiny, however, it becomes apparent that the relationships are often characterized by a striking lack of depth and lack of concern for the other individual as a person. Depth and empathy are lacking, and the borderline individual often vacillates between superficial relationships and intense, dependent relationships that are marred by primitive defenses. The terms *need-fulfilling relationships* and *as-if relationships*, or relationships based on part objects, are appropriate here. Underlying the superficially intact interpersonal relations are internalized object relations that are quite primitive, characterized by unintegrated and contradictory self and object representations.

ADAPTATION TO REALITY

Adaptation to reality is superficially intact, in that the borderline individual may seem of normal appearance and may seem to manifest adequate achievement in work or school. Under close scrutiny, however, the adaptation often appears less than optimal. The underlying ego weaknesses usually make it very difficult for the individual to maintain the adaptation over time. There are certain "exceptional" borderline individuals who can maximize certain strengths and adapt adequately over time, particularly in structured settings. They often do quite well professionally but typically display much more chaos in their social lives. This exceptional group, more than others, seems to seek out intensive psychotherapy.

The Underlying Ego Weaknesses

POOR IMPULSE CONTROL AND POOR FRUSTRATION TOLERANCE

Invariably, the borderline personality displays the combination of poor frustration tolerance and poor impulse control. There is a demand for immediate gratification and a proclivity to act out under stress, frequently combined with a sense of entitlement. Clinically, one finds tendencies toward disruptive anger, drug and alcohol use, and flight from the work or interpersonal situation under stress.

THE TENDENCY TO USE PRIMITIVE EGO DEFENSES

Emphasis here is on the tendency to use primitive ego defenses. In day-to-day functioning, the borderline individual tends to use primitive defenses at least somewhat more than the neurotic; under stress, he tends to rely on these defenses. In Chapter 2 a hierarchy of defenses, including mature, neurotic, immature, borderline, and narcissistic levels, was presented. Primitive defenses are defined as borderline defenses, plus acting out and the narcissistic defenses. In day-to-day functioning the borderline personality, with marked individual variation, uses a combination of neurotic, immature, and borderline defenses. Under stress, there is a marked tendency to rely on the borderline defenses. In marked regressions some narcissistic defenses may be employed as well. Characteristically, the borderline individual does not use the mature defenses.

As noted, Kernberg views the use of the borderline defenses as crucial for both diagnoses and conceptual understanding of the borderline. Although others are not so specific here, agreement is more uniform about the tendency of the borderline to use primitive defenses, especially under stress.

IDENTITY DIFFUSION

The term *identity diffusion* is used here as it is used by Kernberg. It refers to an identity that is not integrated or cohesive but, rather, diffuse—one based on multiple contradictory, unintegrated self images. Correspondingly, there are multiple contradictory, unintegrated object images. A comprehensive view of neither the self nor objects has ever been attained. Because of this, the borderline individual is unable to describe himself or others in a meaningful way. There is a lack of temporal continuity regarding the self and others, along with an overall distortion of the perceptions of self and others.

AFFECTIVE INSTABILITY

A common characteristic of the borderline personality is what might be termed the nonadaptive use of aggression, or affective instability. Thus, the presence of intense affect, usually depressive or hostile; anger as the main affect experienced; and

depressed, lonely, and empty feelings are frequently emphasized. Aggression is not used in constructive, ego-syntonic,
adaptive ways such as sublimations, work, recreation, and
enjoyment. Psychoanalytically, this characteristic is related to a
defect in the neutralization of aggression. Thus, the aggression
often breaks through directly in disruptive ways, such as
outbursts of anger and rage, or is defended in maladaptive ways
and results in other ego-dystonic affect states, such as depression, boredom, and emptiness. Often there are rapid and
dramatic swings from one affect state to another.

This characteristic of affective instability is not emphasized
by Kernberg, yet it is commonly noted in the literature. In fact,
this characteristic seems to be grossly overemphasized by
some, as will be detailed later. Although affective instability is
technically a structural derivative involving both the ego and
the id, it is listed here as one of the four underlying ego
weaknesses in the borderline personality.

Thus, the ego psychological diagnostic approach makes the
diagnosis of borderline personality based on a characteristic
ego profile. The relative ego strengths basically differentiate the
borderline individual from the psychotic, and the underlying
ego weaknesses basically differentiate the borderline individual
from the neurotic. This characteristic ego profile provides a
current, generally accepted summary of the psychodynamic
concept of the borderline personality.

CHAPTER 7

DSM-III and the
Description-oriented Approaches

A number of more descriptive approaches to the borderline condition have emerged in recent years, attempting to establish a description that is simple, reliable, and valid. The emphasis here is on diagnosis rather than psychodynamics. Among these approaches, the work of Gunderson (Gunderson 1977, Gunderson, Carpenter, and Strauss 1975, Gunderson and Kolb 1978, Gunderson and Singer 1975) first emerged as the most widely read. *DSM-III* has recently replaced Gunderson's work as the predominant diagnostic system. This chapter will review the current descriptive approaches to the borderline personality, providing sufficient detail both to permit an understanding of these approaches and to relate them to the more dynamic writings. Because *DSM-III* is now the predominant diagnostic system in psychiatry a more in-depth discussion and critique of this system is presented.

The Research-oriented Approach

In contrast to the psychodynamic approach to the borderline personality typified by Kernberg's work, a second predominant approach has arisen and become increasingly popular in recent years. The second approach in part seems to be a response to concern about the variability of the descriptions offered by the psychodynamically oriented group.

The primary focus here is on symptoms and traits, particularly those that most clearly differentiate the borderline from other groups of patients. Literature reviews, research designs, and statistical methods are employed to try to identify those traits and symptoms. Often long checklists are used to make this differentiation. Basically *DSM-III* can be seen to be an outcome of this approach.

Gunderson and Singer (1975), in a summary of the literature, identified six characteristic features of borderline patients. These included the presence of intense affect, usually depressive or hostile, a history of impulsive behavior, a certain social adaptiveness, brief psychotic experiences under stress, loose thinking in unstructured situations, and interpersonal relations that vacillate between transient superficiality and intense dependency. The authors believed that these features could be identified via the clinical interview, and Gunderson, Kolb, and Austin (1981) later devised a semistructured interview to aid in this pursuit. This Diagnostic Interview for Borderlines (DIB), unlike the structural interview of Kernberg, places major emphasis on history and is easily administered.

Gunderson and Kolb (1978) set out to find those features of the borderline condition that clearly differentiated it from others. Applying sophisticated research designs and statistical analyses, they identified seven items that clearly distinguished the borderline from both neurotic and schizophrenic patients. These seven were not unlike the six of the Gunderson and Singer work. They included low achievement, impulsivity, manipulative suicide attempts, heightened affectivity, mild psychotic episodes, high socialization, and disturbed close relationships. The six characteristic features described by

Gunderson and by Singer clearly correlate with Kernberg's findings and with the ego strengths and weaknesses of the ego psychological approach. The seven items of Gunderson and Kolb are also compatible with Kernberg's descriptions and the ego psychological approach, although the emphasis is slightly different.

A number of other attempts at differentiating the borderline from both neurotic and psychotic patient groups, via behavioral checklists and statistical methods, have appeared. In the original work here, the authors, Grinker, Werble, and Drye (1968), using statistical analyses, identified four features characteristic of all borderline individuals. These included anger as the main and only affect, a defect in affectional relationships, an absence of consistent self-identity, and depression characterizing life. The authors further differentiated four subgroups of borderline individuals: a neurotic border group, an "as-if" group, a psychotic border group, and a core borderline group. The neurotic borderline group was characterized by anxiety and depression, low self-esteem, low confidence, and childlike, clinging interpersonal relationships. This group seems basically to comprise individuals with depressive character structures. The "as-if" group was characterized by stereotyped and stilted but appropriate behavior, easily influenced by others and changing in accordance with others' expectations. Individuals in this group showed little affect or spontaneity, using much isolation and intellectualization. This group is similar to the group of "as-if" characters described by Deutsch (1942). The psychotic borderline group displayed the most inappropriate and maladaptive behavior. Individuals in this group were most deficient in identity formation and reality testing and were vulnerable to brief psychotic episodes under stress. The core borderline group was characterized by a prominence of affect, both angry and depressive, by stormy and vacillating interpersonal relationships, and by inconsistencies in identity. This study was the first to apply a sophisticated research design using statistical methods to the borderline concept. In subdividing the borderline conditions, Grinker and colleagues antedated Meissner's work (1981, 1982–1983,1983), to be discussed later, which views the borderline condition as a spectrum of disorders. Grinker and colleagues emphasized affect more than anyone cited so far, and in this respect anticipated both the work of Klein (1977) and *DSM-III* (1980), also to be discussed shortly.

More recently, Perry and Klerman (1978) reviewed articles on the borderline personality by Knight (1953), Kernberg (1967), Grinker, Werble, and Drye (1968) and Gunderson and Singer (1975), and compiled a checklist of 104 criteria for the diagnosis of the borderline condition. Comparing the four articles using these criteria, they found a striking lack of agreement and thus questioned the legitimacy of the concept of the borderline condition. Even more recently, however, Perry and Klerman (1980), using their previously conducted literature review, constructed a rating scale of 129 items to distinguish borderline patients from other patients. This time, in a statistical comparison of patients who had the "definite" diagnosis of borderline with patients who did not, they found that 81 of the 129 items were significantly more characteristic of the patients diagnosed as borderline than the patients with other diagnoses. Perry and Klerman posited that those 81 items significantly distinguished those patients diagnosed as borderline from those with other diagnoses. They concluded that the diagnostic entity of the borderline was indeed a valid concept.

There seems to be a high degree of overlap in making the diagnosis of borderline personality, whether using the criteria of the ego psychological approach, Kernberg (1981), Gunderson (1982), or Perry and Klerman (1978, 1980). Besides those already mentioned, a number of similar studies (Gunderson 1982), again using sophisticated research designs and statistical analyses, have also demonstrated the existence of a borderline group of patients, clearly distinguishable from both a sicker, psychotic group and a healthier, neurotic group.

The Borderline Personality as a Subgroup of Schizophrenia

A third approach to the borderline patient is subscribed to by a group of genetic researchers who are trying to establish a concept of borderline pathology within the genetic spectrum of schizophrenia. The term *borderline schizophrenia* is applicable here. Symptoms and traits that would establish genetic linkages to schizophrenia are sought within this approach. This approach is related to the research-oriented approach just discussed, in that sophisticated research designs, statistical analyses, easily defined groups, and reliability are emphasized. *DSM-III* is related to this approach, because it basically uses its results to define the schizotypal personality disorder.

Kety, Rosenthal, Wender, and Schulsinger (1968), and Kety, Wender, et al. (1975) are the prominent researchers in this area. Using comprehensive Danish adoptive records, these authors were able to identify a sample of schizophrenic patients who had been adopted shortly after birth. They were also able to locate most of the biological and adopted relatives of these patients and to make detailed comparisons between these groups. In their sample of patients, besides including acute and chronic schizophrenic groups, these authors included a group they called "borderline state." The characteristics of this group of patients included difficulties in thinking, brief periods of cognitive distortion, micropsychosis, depersonalization and derealization, anhedonia, lack of affective involvement, lack of in-depth interpersonal involvement, chaotic sexual adjustment, and multiple neurotic symptoms. The authors included this "borderline" group within their concept of the schizophrenic spectrum, this inclusion being necessary to support the best genetic evidence for chronic schizophrenia. Unfortunately, the results regarding the genetic relationship between this borderline group and the chronic schizophrenic group seem unclear. Depending on how one looks at the data, there is evidence both for and against such a relationship. This study is relevant to the construction of *DSM-III*.

The Borderline Personality as a Subgroup of Affective Disorders

A fourth approach is that of Donald Klein (1977). Klein views many borderline patients as representing a subgroup of the affective disorders. He has described a number of specific syndromes (hysteroid dysphoria, emotionally unstable character disorder, phobic-anxiety reactions, and others) that basically fall within the borderline group by other classifications, and then sought to demonstrate that these syndromes are actually subgroups of affective disorders and respond to antidepressants. Klein believes there is an overemphasis on the psychic structure of the borderline patient, whereas the patient's longitudinal affective status is underemphasized. The condition that Klein describes might well be called the borderline affective disorder.

Klein's approach initially seems incompatible with the psychodynamic approach. However, a specific subgroup of patients diagnosed as having a borderline personality organization via the psychodynamic approach might be especially vulnerable to depressions or suffer superimposed depressions. There is some research (Stone 1977, Akiskal 1981, Pope, Jonas, Hudson, et al. 1983) supporting an overlap of the borderline personality and affective disorders. A relevant preliminary conclusion, in agreement with others (Pope, Jonas, Hudson, et al. 1983), is that these patients demonstrate the two disorders simultaneously, rather than the borderline condition representing a subgroup of affective disorders. The diagnostic system chosen to establish the diagnosis of borderline personality would be highly related to the degree of overlap of borderline and affective disorders. Some systems, such as *DSM-III*, greatly emphasize affective disturbance in their diagnostic criteria, whereas others, such as Kernberg's, do not.

DSM-III

DSM-III is the current official psychiatric nomenclature. The task force involved in producing *DSM-III* (Spitzer, Endicott, and Gibbon 1979) noted two major ways in which the term *borderline* was currently used. The first, similar to that of both Kernberg and Gunderson, defined the borderline as a constellation of relatively enduring features of instability and vulnerability. The second, following the lead of Wender, Kety, and Rosenthal, described the borderline as having certain psychopathological characteristics stable over time and genetically related to the schizophrenia spectrum. Via a review of the literature, and following personal consultations with advocates of these two approaches (including Kernberg, Gunderson, and Wender, Kety, and Rosenthal), the task force created two lists of items, describing the borderline according to each of these two approaches. To the constellation of traits on the list representing the first approach, the term *borderline personality* was assigned; to the second list of traits, the term *schizotypal personality* was given. Support for these separate lists was obtained by statistical analyses of the responses on a questionnaire sent to over 800 psychiatrists. High sensitivity and specificity were demonstrated for each list, although there were a significant number of patients who fulfilled the diagnostic criteria for both lists. These two entities, the borderline and schizotypal personality disorders, were included among the personality disorders in *DSM-III*.

To make the *DSM-III* diagnosis of schizotypal personality disorder, one must demonstrate four of eight items as characteristic of the individual's current and long-term functioning. These items include magical thinking, ideas of reference, social isolation, recurrent illusions, depersonalization and derealization, odd speech, inadequate rapport, and undue social anxiety or hypersensitivity to real or imagined criticism. Most of these items do seem to portray symptoms similar to those evident in mild cases of schizophrenia. A recent research article (Gunderson, Siever, and Spaulding 1983) modified the list of *DSM-III* schizotypal personality characteristics and showed that this modified list was very much in accordance with the borderline characteristics of the patients of Kety, Rosenthal, Wender and associates (Kety et al. 1968, Kety et al. 1975) while clearly distinguishable from the traits of the *DSM-III* borderline personality disorder. In this article the *DSM-III* borderline personality disorder was not thought to be associated with schizophrenia.

The *DSM-III* description of the borderline personality disorder seems more in accordance with the general use of the term *borderline* in psychiatry today. Using a behavior checklist to establish the diagnosis, *DSM-III* basically fits into the

research-oriented approach described in this book. To make
the *DSM-III* diagnosis, one must demonstrate five of eight items
as characteristic of the individual's current and long-term
functioning. These items include impulsivity or unpredictability
in at least two areas that are potentially self-damaging, a pattern
of unstable and intense interpersonal relationships, inappropriate intense anger or lack of control of anger, identity
disturbance, affective instability, intolerance of being alone,
physically self-damaging acts, and chronic feelings of emptiness or boredom. Several differences between these items and
those of the other well-known approaches, as typified by
Kernberg and Gunderson, are readily apparent. Unlike the
conceptualizations of Kernberg and Gunderson, there is no
mention of the vulnerability to brief psychotic episodes or
disorganized thinking under stress. Also, there is no mention of
the positive feature of high level of socialization or superficial
adaptation. In addition, there seems to be an overemphasis on
affective disturbance. Three items (intense anger, affective
instability, and chronic feelings of emptiness or boredom) are
directly relevant to affective disturbance, whereas a fourth
(intolerance of being alone) seems related. Unlike Kernberg's
work, there is no mention of defensive organization, and unlike
Gunderson's, there is no mention of low achievement.

Of these differences, the main reasons for concern are the
omission of defensive functioning, the omission of the vulnerability to brief psychotic episodes and disorganized thinking
under stress, and the overemphasis on affective disturbance. As
noted, Kernberg relies heavily on the level of defensive functioning in making his diagnosis of borderline personality. The
omission of this item in *DSM-III*—and in Gunderson's criteria,
for that matter—might be related to the difficulty in reliably
demonstrating defensive functions on a behavioral checklist. In
addition, there seems to be a deemphasis on ego functioning in
general and defensive functioning in particular in psychiatry
today. A focus on defensive functioning provides invaluable
diagnostic information, and the inclusion of this criterion in a
diagnostic system regarding the borderline personality would
clearly strengthen that system.

Both Kernberg and Gunderson have placed much importance on the vulnerability to brief psychotic regressions under stress in the borderline patient. This vulnerability seems integral to the borderline personality and, as Gunderson (1982) and Gunderson, Siever, and Spaulding (1983) emphasized, should be included in any list of diagnostic criteria. By eliminating this focus on both reality testing and defensive functioning, *DSM-III* has actually eliminated two of the three items most emphasized by Kernberg. These omissions, together with the overemphasis on affective disturbance, could partially explain the overlap of the *DSM-III* borderline personality disorder with affective disorders. This overlap should be reduced by using Gunderson's and especially Kernberg's criteria, although some literature questions this effect (Stone 1977, Akiskal 1981). Nevertheless, it is unclear why so many items reflecting affective disturbance were chosen as part of the diagnostic criteria for *DSM-III*. As has been mentioned previously, despite theoretical differences, there seems to be a high degree of overlap in making the diagnosis of borderline personality, whether using the criteria of Kernberg, Gunderson, or Perry and Klerman. Despite the differences between *DSM-III* and these other sets of criteria, there is preliminary evidence that the *DSM-III* criteria also overlap with the others (Gunderson 1982).

DSM-III, in agreement with Gunderson, views the borderline as one of many distinct personality disorders. Kernberg, on the other hand, views the borderline personality as a level of structural organization, to be differentiated from both neurotic and psychotic levels. Thus, according to Kernberg, the borderline personality can be seen as a supraordinate diagnosis, under which more specific personality disorders would fall. Of the various personality disorders described in *DSM-III*, it seems highly likely that the vast majority of patients diagnosed as evidencing histrionic, narcissistic, or antisocial personality disorders would also meet the diagnostic criteria for the borderline personality. The major studies (Gunderson and Kolb 1978, Perry and Klerman 1980, Gunderson 1982) that have identified the borderline personality as a distinct entity have distinguished it from groups of neurotic and psychotic patients. To date there have been no studies distinguishing the borderline from more specific personality disorders. In fact, some studies (Pope, Jonas, Hudson, et al. 1983) have indicated that making this distinction is no simple task. Thus, Kernberg's approach here seems more in accord with both theoretical considerations and current psychiatric research, than does *DSM-III*.

CONCLUSIONS REGARDING *DSM-III*

DSM-III is significant in that it is the first official nomenclature to embrace the term *borderline*. Using a behavioral checklist, *DSM-III* defines the borderline personality disorder so as to enhance reliability and research value. There are many problems with *DSM-III*, however, from a number of points of view. In comparison with other attempts at diagnosis, there is an obvious overemphasis on affective disturbance, creating a potential overlap diagnostically between the borderline and affective disorders. There is the omission of a diagnostic criterion related to the vulnerability to brief psychotic regressions under stress. There is the more controversial omission of defensive functioning as a diagnostic criterion. The checklist approach takes away from dynamic understanding and makes potentially valuable items such as defensive organization difficult to include. It would be interesting to see if a behavioral checklist could be constructed more in accordance with an ego psychological approach, thus providing more psychodynamic underpinnings. The concept of the borderline personality disorder as one of many distinct personality disorders seems unfounded. The concept of the borderline as a supraordinate diagnosis under which more specific personality disorders fall appears more reasonable.

The Ego Psychological Diagnostic Approach as a Research-oriented Approach

There is no reason why the dynamically oriented approaches cannot be presented in checklist form and then subjected to the research methods just described. Kernberg (Kernberg, Goldstein, Carr, et al. 1981) and Bellak (Bellak, Hurvich, and Gediman 1973) have certainly made efforts in this direction. The ego psychological diagnostic approach to the borderline personality we have outlined is ideally suited to this purpose. It would not be difficult to devise a research project testing the reliability and validity of the approach. The end result would be a descriptive diagnostic system, simple, reliable, and valid, with clear psychodynamic underpinnings. In addition, the psychodynamic underpinnings would be easily described and would represent the current psychodynamic concept of the borderline personality.

A preliminary effort (Goldstein 1984) of this nature has been undertaken. In this study a modification of Bellak's rating system (Bellak, Hurvich, and Gediman 1973) was used to evaluate the patients' ego functioning in the areas of reality testing, thought processes, object relations, adaptation to reality, defensive functioning, impulse control, synthetic functioning, concept of self, and the nonadaptive use of aggression (or affective instability). These ratings were compared with those for a group of 144 hospitalized patients, divided in diagnoses among schizophrenia, borderline personality, and character disorder. Diagnoses of schizophrenia and borderline personality were made in accordance with *DSM-III*. Diagnosis of character disorder was made when the patient was thought to have characterological difficulties that were clear cut but not severe enough to meet the *DSM-III* criteria for borderline personality. The results, statistically significant, differentiated the group of borderline patients from both the more pathological schizophrenic group and the less pathological character disorder group in all areas except the nonadaptive use of aggression (or affective instability) and impulse control. This study was unable to differentiate the borderline patient from either of the other two groups in nonadaptive use of aggression. Subgrouping of the ego function of impulse control demonstrated significant differences between the borderline and the other two groups in some areas of impulse control, but not in others. In accordance with the findings of a past study (Goldstein 1981a), it was concluded that the borderline patient differed in impulse control from those in the other two groups in a qualitative, rather than a quantitative, way. Possible reasons for the findings regarding the nonadaptive use of aggression and impulse control will not be detailed here.

Subgroupings of the ego functions of reality testing, thought processes, and object relations further demonstrated the borderline group to be very similar to the character disorder group in these areas on a superficial level, yet much more disturbed on a deeper level. Except in the area of affective instability, the borderline group in this study was basically identical to the group defined by the ego psychological diagnostic approach. In this study, the borderline group was clearly differentiated from the psychotic by the relative ego strengths of reality testing, thought processes, object relations, and the adaptation to reality. The borderline group was clearly differentiated from the healthier character disorder group by the ego weaknesses of defensive functioning, concept of self, synthetic function, and possibly impulse control. Despite its methodological flaws, this preliminary study does present some evidence that a diagnostic system for the borderline patient can be attained that combines easy description, reliability, and validity with psychodynamic understanding.

CHAPTER 8

The Borderline Spectrum (Meissner)

Meissner (1978a, 1978b, 1981, 1982–1983, 1983) has written a number of fine articles, culminating in a recent book (1984), offering valuable refinements and critiques regarding the borderline personality. He specifically has focused on Kernberg's work, on the one hand acknowledging its predominant and contributive position, and on the other hand offering sophisticated and useful additions and criticisms. Noting the multitude of manifestations of borderline psychopathology, Meissner has experienced difficulty in trying to conceptualize the borderline patient via one unified theory. Correspondingly, he has expressed problems with viewing the borderline personality as a single entity. Meissner (1981, 1982–1983, 1983, 1984) has recently come to the conclusion that the borderline condition can be best thought of as representing a heterogeneous group of patients, represented by a spectrum of levels and degrees of pathological personality functioning. The conditions on the spectrum can be differentiated by several variables, including the quality of object relations, the degree of object constancy, the level of achieved and maintained self-cohesion, the regressive potential, the degree of projective tendency, and the levels of ego and superego structuralization.

Although different in detail, these differentiating variables are not unlike those of the ego psychological diagnostic approach (Goldstein 1982, 1983), discussed in Chapter 6.

Hysterical Continuum

Meissner proposes two large groupings of the borderline condition, each along a continuum of increasing psychopathology. In the first group, which he calls the hysterical continuum, listed in decreasing order of psychopathology, he includes the pseudoschizophrenic group, the psychotic character, the borderline personality proper (or dysphoric personality), and the primitive hysteric. The variables thought to characterize this grouping, as psychopathology increases, are increasing affective lability, decreasing frustration tolerance, increasing tendencies for externalization and acting out, increasing signs of ego weakness, increasing instability of introjective configurations with a corresponding failure in self-cohesion, increasing amounts of primitive pregenital aggression, increasing primitive organization of defenses, increasing susceptibility to regressive pulls, and object relations that are increasingly clingingly dependent and ambivalent, and increasingly susceptible to fears of abandonment and loss. Again, these variables are very similar to those of the ego psychological approach.

Schizoid Continuum

In the second group, which he calls the schizoid continuum, Meissner includes the schizoid personality, the "as-if" personality, the false self organization, and the condition of identity diffusion. The common dilemma of the conditions in this continuum is the powerful need for objects, on the one hand, and the intense fear of closeness or intimacy associated with these objects, on the other hand. Significant relationships expose the self to fears of loss or dissolution. The way in which the patient establishes a self to deal with this dilemma determines the subgroup into which he or she will fit. The schizoid continuum includes a sense of withdrawal and isolation, a rigidity of defenses, and a resistance to regression that distinguishes it from the hysterical continuum. Unlike those in the hysterical continuum, the subgroups here do not seem well differentiated from one another, nor is there a clear sense of a continuum of increasing degrees of psychopathology.

Subgroups of the Hysterical Continuum

The first subgroup of the hysterical continuum is the *pseudo-schizophrenic subgroup*, the most pathological within the hysterical continuum. This subgroup contains patients previously described as pseudoneurotic schizophrenics (Hoch and Polatin 1949, Hoch and Cattell 1959), latent psychotics (Bychowsky 1953), ambulatory schizophrenics (Zilboorg 1941), and latent schizophrenics (American Psychiatric Association 1952). The best known of these descriptions is that of pseudoneurotic schizophrenia by Hoch and Polatin (1949). This group is characterized by pananxiety, panneurosis (multiple neurotic symptoms), and pansexuality. Although these patients superficially appear neurotic according to the original description, on close scrutiny they are revealed to be schizophrenic. If not schizophrenic, this pseudoschizophrenic group is the group most closely bordering on and sharing characteristics with the schizophrenic constellation. Although often hidden behind a façade of adequate superficial social functioning, primary process thinking is invariably found very close to the surface, often during clinical interviewing and certainly on psychological testing. There are frequent failures in reality testing, the presence of diffuse, intense, and chronic anxiety, very poor frustration tolerance and impulse control, and little cohesiveness or stability in the organization of the self. Defensive organization can look neurotic on the surface but shifts rapidly to more primitive patterns. If this group is not basically schizophrenic, it is only one step removed.

The *psychotic character*, best described by Frosch (1964, 1970), is a condition in which the patient's ego capacities are significantly stronger than in the pseudoschizophrenic subgroup. Although these patients share some ego psychological characteristics with psychotics, they differ from psychotic patients in their relative ability to preserve reality testing, their superior object relations, and their capacity for rapid reversibility when regressions do occur. Although there are frequent impairments in the sense of reality and the relationship to reality, reality testing can be maintained for long periods, although it is quite sensitive and vulnerable to reversible regressions under stress. The pseudoschizophrenic, like the psychotic in general (as described in Chapter 2), has to expend energy continuously just to prevent regressions. The psychotic character, in contrast, does not have to make such a constant expenditure of energy yet is very sensitive and vulnerable to reversible regressions under stress. In addition, the self organization in the psychotic character is fragile and not cohesive, and the defensive pattern can be primitive, with an overuse of projective and introjective mechanisms. Meissner believes that a number of the patients described by Kernberg actually fit into this category.

The next condition described by Meissner, the *borderline personality proper* (or *dysphoric personality*), represents a distinct step upward in the developmental scale from the psychotic character. The borderline personality of Meissner does not correspond to Kernberg's condition of the same name (1967, 1975). Kernberg's description of the borderline personality, Meissner believes, applies in part throughout the borderline spectrum, whereas Meissner's borderline personality has a very restricted definition. Probably in an effort to avoid confusion, with the publication of his book (1984), Meissner replaced the term *borderline personality* as used to describe this subgroup with the new term *dysphoric personality*. Meissner's dysphoric personality differs from the psychotic character in its relative resistance to regressions in the area of reality. Whereas the psychotic character is very vulnerable to reversible regressions, the dysphoric personality regresses only under pronounced stress, basically maintaining a consistent

relationship to reality and intact reality testing. An[x]
pervasive and begins to be of a signal variety. O[.]
although not dominating, begin to be eviden[..]
defensive organization, except under acute stress, is simila[.] [.]
that of the neurotic. The predominant area of pathology,
besides the tendency toward regressions under acute stress, is
in the area of identity and the self. The dysphoric personality
does not have a well-integrated concept of himself and others,
displaying a kind of identity diffusion, to use Kernberg's term.
He maintains several different and contradictory pathological
introjective configurations, all available to consciousness.
These include what Meissner calls the victim-introject and the
aggressor-introject, plus narcissistic configurations of grandiosity and inferiority. All these introjective configurations are
well organized, yet there is no integration of these various
configurations to form a cohesive self. These configurations
distort the individual's experiences of interpersonal relations,
yet these patients are able to maintain consistent relationships
to reality and relatively good ego functioning in general.

The *primitive hysteric* is the least pathological entity on the
hysterical continuum. Unlike the dysphoric personality, the
primitive hysteric is able to maintain a cohesive sense of self,
along the lines of what Meissner calls the victim-introject.
These patients seldom regress and are similar to the infantile
personality as described by Kernberg (1967, 1975). They are
characterized by emotional lability, poor impulse control, the
need to be loved and to be the center of attention, the quality of
helplessness, and sexual provocativeness and promiscuity,
along with polymorphous perverse sexual fantasies. They easily
form overinvolved and childlike relationships of a demanding,
clinging, and aggressive nature. In general, there are many
pregenital and oral problems, along with a reduced capacity for
stable interpersonal relationships.

Meissner believes that Zetzel's second- and third-grade
hysterics (1968) fit in this subgroup, with her fourth grade
(most pathological) fitting the description of the psychotic
character. It is unclear what Meissner has in mind here.
Zetzel's grade-two hysterics clearly do not fit the description
given here, appearing substantially healthier and unlikely to fit

any definition of borderline personality. Including even Zetzel's grade-three hysterics within this subgroup seems questionable.

Subgroups of the Schizoid Continuum

Meissner's schizoid continuum is somewhat confusing and does not provide the same potential for clarification as the hysterical continuum. Its subgroups are not well differentiated, nor do they provide a continuum of increasing degrees of psychopathology. The patients in the various subgroups of the schizoid continuum use different means to avoid exposing the "real self" to potential loss or dissolution via significant relationships. Basically, the schizoid personality avoids and withdraws from interpersonal activities to protect the self. The false self (Winnicott 1965) offers a compliant façade for interpersonal activities while protecting the withdrawn "true self." Similarly, the "as-if" personality (Deutsch 1942) offers a superficial, transient, imitative involvement with others while protecting the "true self" by minimizing meaningful and enduring commitments. The individual using identity diffusion offers many conflicting identities, keeping the "true self" ambiguous. The subgroups of the schizoid continuum do seem to fit into the borderline group. Yet it is not clear that they represent different entities, rather than different ways of viewing the same entity.

Critique

Meissner's view of the borderline conditions as a heterogeneous spectrum of levels and degress of pathological personality functioning seems to be an excellent and potentially very useful conceptualization. His grouping of this spectrum into two continua, however, one hysterical and the other schizoid, seems somewhat artificial and unclear. Although the subgroups of the hysterical continuum are well differentiated from one another and offer much potential, the subgroups of the schizoid continuum are poorly differentiated and possibly represent merely different ways of viewing the same entity. The pseudoschizophrenic group, the psychotic character, and the dysphoric personality of the hysterical continuum represent well-described and distinct subgroups. There seems to be too large a psychopathological leap, however, from the psychotic character to Meissner's dysphoric personality. Another entity is needed to fill the gap between these two. The dysphoric personality could then stand at the end of the continuum, avoiding the very confusing entity of the primitive oral hysteric.

If we place Meissner's dysphoric personality at the end point, the entire hysterical continuum can be characterized by two core problems: the difficulty in the integration of the self and the formation of a stable identity, and the proclivity for regressions in reality testing under stress. This grouping would put Meissner in closer theoretical proximity to Kernberg, who places his primary emphasis on these two problem areas, together with the use of primitive defenses. Such an approach would also offer a simple, unifying understanding of the entire continuum. This understanding is particularly lost if the primitive oral hysteric, displaying neither of the two "core problems," is included. With the addition of a subgroup between the psychotic character and the dysphoric personality, possibly the subgroups of the schizoid continuum could fit into the hysterical continuum. Thus, it would be possible to recast Meissner's spectrum into one continuum, including four subgroups, all characterized by the two core problems cited. Although Meissner's idea of a heterogeneous spectrum of levels and degrees of pathological personality functioning seems potentially very useful, the conceptualization and differentiation of the different continua and subgroups seem to need further work and refinement.

CHAPTER 9

The Borderline Patients of Abend, Porder, and Willick

Abend, Porder, and Willick (1983) discussed the concept of the borderline patient with about twenty-five of their colleagues over a four-year period. Four patients, thought to fulfill the "descriptive features of borderline patients" as defined by this group, were studied in detail. All these patients had completed "classical" analyses at least somewhat successfully. A number of observations and conclusions were drawn based on an in-depth look at these analyses. Many of these conclusions vary considerably from what has been thus far presented.

Descriptive Features

The descriptive features offered by Abend and colleagues represent a compilation of "noncontroversial phenomeno-logical" items taken from a review of the literature of Deutsch (1942), Knight (1953), Gitelson (1958), Frosch (1964), Stone (1954), and Kernberg (1966, 1967). The eleven descriptive features are as follows.

1. The pathology tends to invade the entire character structure and to be relatively stable.
2. Although the relationship to reality is impaired, as evidenced in perceptual distortions, poor judgment, and states of disturbed sense of reality, there remains either rapid reversibility of the defects or the persistent intactness of some degree of reality testing.
3. Interpersonal relations are infantile, with egocentricity, demandingness, and exploitiveness, and sometimes with passivity, overidealization, and submissiveness.
4. The life history is likely to reveal evidence of severe impairment.
5. Polysymptomatic clinical pictures, covering almost the entire range of neurotic symptomatology, are presented.
6. There may be psychotic fragments, primitive wishes and fantasies, and primary process thinking.
7. Narcissistic features are emphasized by many theorists.
8. Atypical, intense, early transference reactions occur. These are characterized by unusually strong affects and contradictory, unintegrated attitudes toward the analyst, and an inability to understand the unrealistic feelings and attitudes toward the analyst.
9. The prominence of aggressive conflicts is noted by some.
10. There is substantial disturbance in the area of affect, characterized by inappropriate, labile, absent, false, overintense, and poorly controlled emotion.
11. Specific and characteristic countertransference reactions are evoked.

Regarding items 6, 7, and 9, there are some differences of opinion.

Conclusions of Abend and Colleagues

Observations and conclusions were grouped into a number of categories.

Object relations. The four patients were noted to suffer from a number of serious disturbances. All patients had made

strong identifications with their very disturbed parents, both
from early childhod and from later phases of development. The
object relations of the patients were characterized by marked
sadomasochistic features and profound degrees of narcissism.
All patients showed evidence of severe oedipal problems rather
than primarily pregenital ones. Although gross psychotic
distortions of self-object differentiation were not seen, the
frequent projection of aggression, envy, greed, homosexuality,
and other characteristics contributed to some distortion in the
differentiation of self and object. All patients demonstrated
severe reactions to separations, and all showed evidence of
superego conflicts in their object relations.

Reality testing. The severe distortions of self-object differentiation typical of psychoses were absent. In part because
of the frequent use of projections, however, the patients' views
of actual people and situations, and of the world in gereral,
showed considerable disturbance. This kind of defect in reality
testing, not so global as in the psychotic, was nevertheless
observed regularly, showed significant improvement with
analysis, and was thought to be basically defensive. The authors
hypothesized that conflicts in both preoedipal and oedipal
development played a role in the problems in reality testing.

Defenses. The patients employed a plethora of defenses,
including those typically termed higher level, mature, and
neurotic. Repression was commonly used, although in acute
regressive states formerly repressed material often reemerged.
Despite the variety of defenses used, certain ones were most
prevalent. These included projection, denial, acting out, identification with the aggressor, the use of one drive derivative to
defend against another, and sadomasochistic libidinal regression. These defenses were particularly difficult to modify,
despite much effort. The authors disagreed with Kernberg's
finding of specific . primitive defenses associated with the
borderline personality. They found his conceptualization of
splitting and projective identification of little value, and in
general did not find it helpful to categorize defenses hier-
archically. They concluded that they could not differentiate
their "borderline" patients from other patients on the basis of
defenses alone.

Transference and techniques. The patients tended to develop intense transference reactions almost from the beginning of treatment. There was an unusual tendency to act out these transferences, both in and out of the treatment. Sadomasochistic transferences, involving much projection, developed in all patients. A relative failure to accept the "as-if" quality of the transference and the insistence on literal gratifications from the analyst were characteristic. Conflict over loss and narcissistic pathology were regularly involved in the transference. The transference was not thought to reflect early ego states or to be traceable to early specific developmental deficiencies. Instead, transference behavior was understood as deriving from unconscious conflicts that expressed and defended against drive derivatives and painful affects. Countertransference problems were usually intense, related to the analyst's feeling attached, confused, helpless, and frustrated.

Recommended technique was in marked contrast to that of Kernberg, and that of Rinsley and Masterson, to be discussed later. The authors saw little value in confronting the patient's contradictory attitudes during assessment interviews. They disagreed with the selective focus on the negative transference and took issue with an emphasis on aggressive over libidinal conflicts. They disagreed with the suggestion of avoiding genetic interpretations early in the treatment, believing that these interpretations, when possible, were very helpful. They did not advocate understanding and interpreting material in any preplanned manner. Instead, their basic therapeutic approach was similar to that used with healthier patients. No special techniques were believed to be needed or recommended. Thus, psychoanalysis was seen as feasible for some borderline patients.

Etiology. The authors believed that special difficulties arising from specific phases of development could not and should not be implicated in the borderline patient. Instead, they posited that all phases of development, including the oedipal, were involved. They did not view the aggressive drive as playing a larger causative role than the libidinal. In addition, they saw no evidence to implicate constitutional factors. The authors believed prevalent theories of causation to be either overly simplistic or insufficiently sustained.

An overall conclusion was that the term *borderline* represented neither a specific diagnostic entity nor a discrete, recognizable syndrome. Rather, it referred in a nonspecific, descriptive way to a large and varied group of patients. These patients were sicker than the typical neurotic yet not as severely disturbed as the psychotic. Thus, the term *borderline* was seen as a loose supraclassification subsuming a large, heterogeneous group of patients. This group suffered from a wide variety of conflicts, caused by complex admixtures of psychopathology from all stages of psychic development.

These findings of Abend, Porder and Willick are based on an in-depth study of the successful analyses of four "borderline" patients. The fact that these patients were able to do so well in analysis is noteworthy in itself. Because of the small select group studied, the authors caution against extending their findings to borderline patients in general. Yet at times they seem to generalize themselves. It is necessary to understand why the findings of Abend and colleagues vary considerably from those regarding borderline patients presented so far. Closer comparison of the findings of Abend and co-workers with the ego psychological diagnostic criteria (Goldstein 1982, 1983), previously presented, will be undertaken.

Abend and Colleagues Versus the Ego Psychological Diagnostic Approach

As we have noted, the ego psychological approach characterizes the borderline personality as evidencing four relative ego strengths and four underlying ego weaknesses. We will first look at the findings of Abend and colleagues concerning what the ego psychological approach considers to the four relative ego strengths of the borderline personality.

1. *Reality testing.* Abend and colleagues emphasize multiple defects in this area, yet the defects they describe seem milder than some of those focused on by the ego psychological criteria. There are at least two important kinds of defects regarding impaired reality testing. The first kind of defect, more global and most commonly described, is the inability

to distinguish internal stimuli from external stimuli, corresponding to the inability to differentiate self from object representations. This defect is most readily observable in psychotic symptoms such as delusions and hallucinations. A second, more subtle, defect involves current distortions of external reality based on one's internalized past. Here the persistence of infantile fantasies and infantile self and object representations causes distortions in present-day reality. This second type of defect in reality testing is much more common and benign than the first. Abend and colleagues focus on the second, "lesser" defect. Actual regressions to psychosis, characterized by self-object dedifferentiation, are uncharacteristic of their patients. In contrast, the ego psychological approach focuses on both types of reality distortion. The division of reality testing into two types of defects is simplistic compared with the elaborations of this ego function by Abend and co-workers, yet this division is helpful in comparing their findings with the ego psychological diagnostic criteria.

2. *Thought processes.* There is little disagreement between the two approaches.
3. *Interpersonal relations.* The ego psychological approach clearly emphasizes the need-fulfilling, part-object, preoedipal aspects of interpersonal relations. Abend and colleagues give equal attention to other disturbances. These include oedipal problems, sadomasochistic relationships, superego conflicts, and narcissistic problems.
4. There is basically no disagreement regarding *adaptation to reality*, although Abend and co-workers emphasize impairment whereas the ego psychological approach emphasizes superficial strength.

We can compare the findings concerning the four underlying ego weaknesses of the ego psychological position as follows:

5. In contrast to the ego psychological approach, Abend and colleagues do not emphasize problems in *frustration tolerance* and *impulse control.*
6. Abend and co-workers take a view of *defenses* very different from that of the ego psychological approach. They do not

believe in the concept of primitive as opposed to mature defenses, or in the classification of defenses into a hierarchy. Thus, they certainly do not perceive the borderline individual as having a proclivity to use primitive defenses. *Splitting* and *projective identification* are viewed as perplexing terms, generally creating confusion rather than clarification. Their "borderline" patients were perceived as using a plethora of defenses, including ones commonly viewed as mature and neurotic as well as ones usually viewed as more primitive. Despite this approach, Abend and co-workers do single out certain defenses as most characteristic of their patients: projection, denial, acting out, identification with the aggressor, the use of one drive derivative to defend against another, and sadomasochistic regression.

In contrast, the ego psychological approach uses the concept of a hierarchy of defenses and holds that the borderline patient has the tendency to use more primitive defenses, both in day-to-day functioning and under stress. Although the borderline individual typically uses a wide variety of neurotic defenses in addition to the more primitive ones, he or she seldom uses the so-called mature defenses. It is the *proclivity* to use primitive defenses that distinguishes the borderline from patients more neurotic. The typical primitive defenses noted are similar to those described by Kernberg: splitting, primitive idealization, projection, denial, omnipotence, devaluation, acting out, and, under acute regressions, fusion and dedifferentiation. The concept of projective identification is questioned, as it is by Abend and co-workers, although the concept of splitting is found useful.

Thus, both Abend's group and the ego psychological approach recognize the variety of defenses employed by the borderline. Both also note characteristic defenses, called "primitive" in the ego psychological approach and viewed as at least somewhat primitive by Abend and colleagues. Invoking the concept of the hierarchy of defenses, one can say that the defenses Abend and colleagues emphasize, although primitive, are somewhat higher level than those emphasized in the ego psychological approach. Also, the

range of defenses described by Abend and co-workers is
greater, extending into the mature level.

7. *Identity diffusion*, a core concept in the ego psychological
approach, is omitted entirely by Abend and colleagues.

8. *Affective instability*. Abends's group and the ego psychological approach seem basically in agreement.

What is most conspicuous in this comparison is that two of
the four weaknesses listed in the ego psychological conceptualization (frustration tolerance and impulse control, and
identity diffusion) are not even noted by Abend and colleagues.
In addition, these authors generally describe their patients as
functioning on a somewhat higher defensive level than that
described in the ego psychological approach. Concerning
interpersonal relations, Abend and co-workers focus more on
disturbances often associated with more neurotic individuals.
Although they emphasize multiple defects in reality testing,
these defects do not include self-object dedifferentiation under
stress, emphasized more in the ego psychological diagnostic
approach.

Critique

The patients of Abend, Porder, and Willick, although evidencing
severe psychopathology, are nevertheless healthier than the
group deemed borderline by the ego psychological approach.
Whether the former group actually fits into the borderline
category depends on one's classification. One possibility is that
this group, although it includes patients with severe character
pathology and some borderline features, does not clearly fit
into the borderline category. Another possibility is that these
patients fulfill the borderline criteria, but barely. If one thinks
in terms of a continuum, these patients would be grouped on
the healthy end of it. If one thinks in terms of subgroups, these
patients would constitute one of the healthiest of the borderline
classification. Kernberg, when presented with two of the four
patients of this group, deemed them both to be borderline

personalities. Given the conclusions just presented, this seems puzzling.

The work of Abend, Porder, and Willick is a major contribution to the field. It provides an in-depth look, descriptively, dynamically, and psychotherapeutically, at a very disturbed group of patients, the successful analyses of whom must be considered noteworthy. There does seem to be a significant difference between the patients that Abend and colleagues describe and a more disturbed group to whom the term *borderline* is usually applied. Thus, one must be very cautious not to generalize the findings of these authors to this larger group of borderline patients.

CHAPTER 10

Split Object Relations, the Holding Introject, and Shifting Levels of Psychological Functioning

In this chapter several additional ways of conceptualizing the borderline individual will be reviewed. First, the work of Rinsley (1977, 1978) and Masterson (1972, 1976, 1978) on the evolution of the split object relations unit and its connection to early interpersonal interactions between parents and child will be examined. Then, Adler and Buie's concept of the holding introject and its deficiency in borderline individuals (Adler 1981, 1985, Adler and Buie 1979, Buie and Adler 1982–1983) will be discussed. Finally, Gunderson's model of shifting levels of psychological functioning (1984), related to both Rinsley and Masterson's and Adler and Buie's work, will be examined.

The Split Object Relations Unit
(Rinsley and Masterson)

Rinsley (1977, 1978) and Masterson (1972, 1976, 1978) are basically in agreement with Kernberg and with the ego psychological approach to the borderline personality. They add to Kernberg's work by focusing on an area that Kernberg minimizes, that of early interpersonal experience. Their focus is on what actually transpires between the potential borderline child and the parents in the early years of life.

According to Rinsley and Masterson, the mother, often a borderline personality herself, and deriving much gratification from the symbiotic involvement with the child, withdraws her emotional availability when the child begins to make an effort to separate and individuate. This process peaks at the rapprochement subphase (age 16 to 25 months) of the separation-individuation period, a timing in accordance with Mahler's writings (1971). Concomitant with the emotional withdrawal of the mother at this time is the absence and unavailability of the father. The child is presented with the dilemma of being faced with a rejecting, disapproving, and withdrawing (bad) mother if he strives for age-appropriate growth, or an approving, rewarding, and comforting (good) mother if he remains dependent, passive, and compliant. In response to this dilemma, the child internalizes what Rinsley and Masterson have termed the "split object relations unit." This split object relations unit is composed of two part units, each consisting of three parts, as follows:

Withdrawing or Rejecting Part Unit

1. Representation of mother: attacking, critical, and withdrawing when child strives for age-appropriate growth
2. Representation of self: inadequate, helpless, bad
3. Affect: anger and frustration, covering depression related to the abandonment of the mother

Rewarding Part Unit

1. Representation of mother: supportive and approving when child remains dependent, passive, and compliant
2. Representation of self: passive, compliant, good
3. Affect: feeling good, gratified

It is the persistence of the split object relations unit that leads to the psychopathology associated with the borderline personality. This psychopathology includes the reinforcement of splitting and other primitive defenses, the inhibition of the normal separation–individuation process, the incomplete separation of self and object representations, the lack of libidinal object constancy, the inability to mourn, the lack of normal developmental phase specificity, and stunted ego growth. The psychotherapeutic strategy related to this theoretical presentation will be described later, in the section on psychotherapy.

There are several questions frequently asked about Rinsley and Masterson's work. One is how often the early interpersonal relations of the potential borderline individual and his mother are actually in accordance with the interpersonal theory. A second question concerns the specificity of the timing of the interactions to the rapprochement subphase of the separation–individuation period. Even if the outlines of the interpersonal theory are accurate, the question arises as to how this timing can be so precise. Because of these issues, some disagree with aspects of Rinsley and Masterson's work; others believe that their work applies only to a small subgroup of borderline patients. We can view Rinsley and Masterson's work as providing a framework for understanding the early interpersonal development of some borderline individuals.

The Holding Introject (Adler and Buie)

Adler and Buie (Adler 1981, 1985, Adler and Buie 1979, Buie and Adler 1982–1983) use the term *borderline* to refer to a group of patients best described as fitting into Meissner's subgroup of the dysphoric personality (1984). Relying somewhat on the work of Winnicott (1953, 1965, 1969), they hypothesize a deficit in a specific kind of introject, the holding introject, as a core deficit in the borderline patient. According to this approach, the formation of holding introjects is quantitatively inadequate in the borderline patient, and those

formed are unstable and subject to regressive loss of function.

For the infant and child to gain significant autonomy, two
qualities of experience are essential. The first is narcissistic,
related to feelings of personal value; the second is "holding and
soothing." Good-enough mothering in early life usually provides essential holding and soothing. With time the holding and
soothing provided by the parents is internalized, first as holding
introjects and then as psychotic structure. The holding introjects
are lacking in the borderline individual because of the absence
of good-enough mothering in the phases of separation–individuation. Because of this lack, the individual must depend in
an ongoing way on external objects to provide the needed
holding and soothing. The term *self-object* is used to describe
these external objects. The holding self-object is crucial for
providing essential holding and soothing for the borderline
individual; it is needed for the maintenance of psychological
integrity.

The borderline individual can usually maintain sufficient
interaction with holding self-objects to avoid intense separation
anxiety. When there is a disturbance in the holding self-objects,
however, rage can easily ensue, with a forthcoming regression. The regression can involve the loss of the functional use of
the holding self-objects, together with the loss of the memory
bases for these self-objects. At this time separation anxiety
comes to the fore. Adler and Buie use the term *aloneness* to
describe the feeling associated with this separation anxiety.
Aloneness is a very painful feeling, akin to a kind of deadness or
inner emptiness, or a sense of void. With regression, the
separation anxiety can lead to annihilation anxiety, or anxiety
related to the loss of self and psychic structure. When the
borderline individual feels deprived of her holding self-objects,
she seeks ways to regain these self-objects. Under the sway of
regression, fusion and incorporation are used to aid in this
task. This in itself presents a threat of destruction to the self
and/or the self-object, however, and is not a solution. The
borderline individual is thus faced with the dilemma of risking
acute separation anxiety and even annihilation anxiety by
losing the self-objects, or risking destruction of the self and/or

self-object by attempting to retain the self-object via fusion and incorporation.

Psychotherapy with the borderline individual as advocated by Adler and Buie first addresses this core deficit, the lack of the holding introject. Both the concept of deficiency in holding introjects, and the psychotherapeutic focus on this deficiency, seem of clear clinical value in the treatment of a large number of borderline individuals.

Gunderson's Levels of Psychological Functioning

In an approach that corresponds somewhat to the work of Rinsley and Masterson and clearly to that of Adler and Buie, Gunderson (1984) conceptualizes the clinical characteristics of the borderline personality as fluctuating in accordance with his relationship to major objects. Gunderson defines *major object* simply as any significant current relationship perceived as necessary. In this context Gunderson describes three levels of psychological functioning.

Level I corresponds to a time when a major object is present and supportive. This situation corresponds to the libidinal availability of the mother in Rinsley and Masterson's terms and to the presence of the holding introject in the form of a self-object in Adler and Buie's terms. Here the borderline patient demonstrates his best level of functioning. Depressive, bored, and lonely features predominate, along with passivity, difficulty with initiating, and difficulty with sharing. Concern over controlling and being controlled are of prime importance. The dilemma of both needing and fearing the major object is clearly present. At this level the patient appears integrated although compliant and is able to work collaboratively with an active therapist.

Level II corresponds to a time when a major object is present but frustrating, and when there is a fear of the loss of this object. This situation corresponds to a fear of "abandonment" in Rinsley and Masterson's terms, and to the occurence of "aloneness" in Adler and Buie's terms. Here anger predominates. This anger is often modified to lessen fears of losing the object, and sometimes takes the form of sarcasm, demandingness, argumentativeness, and manipulative suicide attempts. Devaluation is used when the patient attempts to deny the value of the major object and thus the fear associated with its potential loss. Manipulation is employed in attempts to retain the major object. Sometimes the anger is projected onto the object, with an ensuing paranoid stance. The clinical characteristics of the borderline patient associated with Level II become activated in the treatment context only when the therapist is seen as a major object. It is at this level that the critical events of psychotherapy take place.

Level III corresponds to a time when a major object is perceived as absent. This situation corresponds to "abandonment" in Rinsley and Masterson's terms, and to the most acute separation anxiety or annihilation anxiety in Adler and Buie's terms. Here the borderline patient is at his worst. Brief psychotic episodes, panic states, and defensive efforts to stave off these states predominate. These defensive efforts include drug and alcohol use, dangerous and impulsive activity, promiscuity, dissociative episodes, and acts of self-mutilation. Psychoticlike depressions with nihilistic fears can occur. All the phenomena of this level are viewed as ways of dealing with the perceived loss of the object and the subsequent aloneness and anxiety. According to Gunderson, these phenomena are usually not in evidence within the psychotherapy itself but are often precipitants for seeking treatment or for hospitalization.

Gunderson provides a useful way of looking at the changing levels of clinical phenomenology of borderline individuals. Although he emphasizes descriptive aspects, his conceptualization is clearly psychodynamically based. The changes in phenomenology are not related to changes in core issues for the borderline individual but, rather, to regressive changes in defensive patterns, related to stress. In this regard, Gunderson's conceptualization is related to that of Kernberg. Gunderson integrates descriptive and psychodynamic frameworks and relates his work usefully to that of Kernberg, Rinsley and Masterson, and Adler and Buie.

PART THREE

Differential Diagnosis

CHAPTER 11

Problems of Differential Diagnosis

The diagnosis of borderline personality, as well as the differential diagnosis, basically depends on the system used to define the term *borderline*. This book has emphasized a diagnostic system that places all individuals into one of three large groupings: the normal-neurotic, the borderline, and the psychotic. A more controversial fourth large grouping, the narcissistic, will be proposed in the next chapter. Each of these groupings is characterized by a distinct underlying structural configuration, consisting of a specific pattern of ego and superego functioning along with a specific pattern of instinctual drive organization. The pattern of ego functioning, described in the form of a profile or inventory of ego functions, by itself is sufficient to establish a differential diagnosis among the large groupings. A first-line diagnosis made in accordance with these groupings provides information invaluable for conceptual understanding, prognostic considerations, and therapeutic planning.

Even with the use of the most elaborate diagnostic systems, many individuals remain difficult to diagnose. Many people simply do not fit clearly into one category or another. There will be many individuals who will be on the "border," between borderline and neurosis or between borderline and psychosis. Likewise, there will be individuals who seem to fit into the narcissistic grouping but for whom this diagnosis cannot be made with certainty. Furthermore, each of the large diagnostic groupings will contain a great variety of people, with widely different personalities and widely different behaviors.

The goal remains to make as accurate a diagnosis as possible. To this end, a thorough evaluation of the individual is always in order. After this evaluation, it is legitimate to claim that a particular person remains a diagnostic enigma. This chapter differentiates the borderline from other diagnostic groupings. However the ubiquity of individual variation must be kept in mind.

The Borderline Ego Profile

Using the ego psychological diagnostic approach, the borderline personality has been presented as having an ego profile characterized by four relative ego strengths and four underlying ego weaknesses. A detailed look at the entire ego profile is of most value when making a differential diagnosis. The relative ego strengths, however, especially reality testing and thought processes, are most helpful in differentiating the borderline from the more psychotic individual. Analogously, the underlying weaknesses, especially the proclivity to use primitive ego defenses and the syndrome of identity diffusion, are most helpful in differentiating the borderline from the basically neurotic individual. The narcissistic individual is differentiated from the borderline by a subtly yet distinctly different ego profile, to be elaborated on later.

The Borderline Personality and the Psychotic

In differentiating between the borderline personality and the psychotic, the prime focus is on reality testing. The borderline individual is characterized by basically intact reality testing, but with a definite vulnerability and propensity to regression in this area under stress. It is the "usual" intactness that differentiates the borderline patient from the psychotic. The psychotic is characterized by a more constant and global defect in reality testing. Although the difference between the borderline individual and the psychotic in this area is usually obvious, difficulties can arise with some psychotic individuals who are able to conceal their psychopathology in reality testing. A basically psychotic individual either constantly demonstrates some evidence of distortion in reality testing or, at best, must continuously expend energy to prevent these distortions from surfacing. In contrast, the borderline individual, although clearly vulnerable to regression, does not need to expend energy constantly to maintain this ego function. In this discussion, reality testing is conceptualized in its most usual way, that is, as the ability to distinguish internal from external stimuli. More subtle defects in reality testing, related to the distortion of present-day reality based on the infantile past, are thought to be much more widespread and much less helpful in differentiating the borderline individual from the psychotic.

A focus on thought processes can also be useful in differentiating the borderline patient from the psychotic. The former typically uses secondary process thinking but shows a possible vulnerability to regression to primary process thinking either under stress or in unstructured situations. A more consistent use of primary process thinking usually indicates a psychotic process. Prior to *DSM-III*, when the diagnosis of schizophrenics was generally made according to the conceptions of Bleuler, the positive demonstration of a thought disorder was thought to be pathognomonic for schizophrenia. Other psychoses, such as depression, were then thought to be characterized by the absence of such a defect. Recent psychiatric research (Pope and Lipinski 1978, Pope, Lipinski, and Cohen, et al. 1980, Procci 1976), as noted, has indicated that the presence of a thought disorder is not necessarily pathognomonic for schizophrenia; a thought disorder can also be found in other psychoses. In making the differential diagnosis between the borderline personality and the psychotic, the occurence of such psychopathology, if consistent, can be taken as a certain indication of a psychotic process, although the psychotic will certainly not always be characterized by the consistent presence of a thought disorder.

Focus on reality testing and thought processes is most crucial in differentiating the borderline patient from the psychotic. Along with differences in these areas, the psychotic often shows more problems than the borderline individual in both interpersonal relations and adaptation to reality. Like the borderline patient, there is usually poor impulse control and poor frustration tolerance, identity diffusion, and affective instability. The typical defensive pattern of the psychotic includes a combination of neurotic, immature, borderline, and narcissistic defenses in day-to-day functioning, with a proclivity to the use of narcissistic defenses under stress. The greater use of the narcissistic defenses distinguishes the psychotic from the borderline individual.

The Borderline Personality and the Neurotic

The underlying ego weaknesses are most helpful in differentiating the borderline individual from the neurotic. Among these weaknesses, the tendency to use primitive ego defenses and the syndrome of identity diffusion seem of most importance. The neurotic uses mainly neurotic and mature defenses in day-to-day functioning, accentuating certain specific neurotic defenses under stress. There may be some acting out, but otherwise there is little use of lower-level defenses, except sporadically under obvious stress. This typical pattern is in marked contrast to that of the borderline patient, who has a much greater propensity to use the borderline defenses, both in day-to-day functioning and under stress. Additionally, the neurotic presents a clearly integrated, cohesive, and stable sense of self and a similarly integrated, cohesive, and stable sense of objects. Others are viewed as complex individuals, clearly having needs and desires of their own. Thus, the syndrome of identity diffusion is clearly absent in the neurotic. In essence, the basically neurotic individual is characterized by good reality testing, secondary process thinking, good interpersonal relations, good adaptation to reality, good impulse control and frustration tolerance, defenses typically characterized as neurotic or higher level, a stable identity, and affective stability. The level of interpersonal relations and adaptation to reality may vary somewhat. In addition, there can be some slippage in frustration tolerance and impulse control, as well as in affective stability. Marked deviation in any of the other areas should clearly call into question the diagnosis of neurosis.

There is a certain group of individuals who display difficulties in impulse control and frustration tolerance, together with affective instability. These individuals typically use much acting out and may use some of the typical borderline defenses. Excepting these characteristics, the ego profiles of these individuals are in the neurotic range. This group is on the border between borderline and neurotic. Meissner would place these people in the borderline group, in the subgroup of the dysphoric personality. The ego psychological diagnostic approach would include these individuals in the borderline group only if the tendency to use the lower-level defenses was marked, or if there was some relative weakening in reality testing or thought processes. Usually one wants to see both the proclivity to use primitive ego defenses and the syndrome of identity diffusion to substantiate the diagnosis of borderline personality.

The Borderline Personality and the Narcissistic Personality

The differentiation of the borderline and the narcissistic personalities, along with the issue of whether the narcissistic personality is a subgroup of the borderline, remains controversial and confusing. The two predominant experts, Kernberg and Kohut, are not in agreement here. Kohut (1966, 1968, 1971, 1977) classifies the borderline personality with the psychotic and clearly differentiates this group from the narcissistic personality. Kernberg (1970, 1974, 1975, 1980a), in contrast, divides the narcissistic personality into three groups, one of which clearly falls into the borderline group and two of which do not. Although it is probably true that a number of individuals with characteristics of the narcissistic personality do fall into the borderline group, there appears to be a group of narcissistic patients with ego profiles somewhat similar to the borderline profile yet subtly but distinctly different under close scrutiny. This group of individuals includes both Kohut's narcissistic personalities and Kernberg's "healthier" narcissistic personalities. It is for this group of individuals that a fourth level of psychic functioning, the narcissistic level, is hypothesized. This narcissistic level clearly falls between the neurotic and the borderline in the degree of psychopathology.

The most striking difference between the narcissistic personality and the borderline is in the area of identity diffusion. Instead of an unintegrated and unstable identity, the narcissistic personality has an integrated although pathological identity based on a grandiose self. This identity, although pathological, is basically stable and cohesive and resists disruptive fragmentation. Reality testing, impulse control and frustration tolerance, and stability of affects are all relatively stronger than in the borderline personality. As in the borderline personality, these functions are sensitive to regression. In the narcissistic personality, however, rather than being global, this sensitivity is limited to the area of narcissistic vulnerability, as we will describe in the next chapter. Interpersonal relations, intact superficially, are maintained to a better degree than in the borderline individual yet are nonetheless distorted by narcissistic configurations. Adaptation to reality is better than in the borderline personality, whereas thought processes remain intact. Defenses used by the narcissistic personality can be similar to those employed by borderline individuals. They certainly include primitive idealization, omnipotence, devaluation, and splitting.

The Borderline Personality, *DSM-III*, and Personality Disorders

The concept of the borderline personality emphasized in this book is that of a supraordinate, or first-level, diagnostic group, under which a number of more specific diagnoses fall. The borderline group is differentiated in this approach by its distinct underlying structural configuration, which differs from that in three other large groups, the neurotic, the psychotic, and the narcissistic. This diagnostic approach is in marked contrast to the more descriptive approach of *DSM-III*. *DSM-III* views the borderline as one of a number of distinct personality disorders and attempts to differentiate this category from the other personality disorders. Many problems arise when this task is undertaken, however; in essence, this differentiation cannot be made adequately. Major studies (Gunderson and Kolb 1978, Perry and Klerman 1980, Gunderson 1982) have been able to identify the borderline personality as a distinct entity and to distinguish it from groups of both neurotic and psychotic patients. There have not yet been studies distinguishing the borderline from more specific personality disorders; some studies (Pope, Jonas, Hudson, et al. 1983), in fact, have indicated how difficult this task would be.

Many personality disorders, along with some of the symptomatic neuroses, fall within the borderline group. Included here are most impulse-ridden characters, most inadequate personalities, some schizoid personalities, some narcissistic personalities, some phobic neurotics, most paranoid personalities, and most antisocial personalities. Some alcoholics and many drug abusers also fall into the borderline group. A number of the personality disorders overlap with the *DSM-III* borderline personality and can be considered part of the borderline group. These include many of the paranoid, schizotypal, histrionic, narcissistic, and antisocial personalities.

The Borderline Personality and the Schizophrenic

The borderline personality is viewed in this book as a specific, stable pathological personality organization, characterized by a specific kind of underlying structural configuration. The schizophrenic is viewed as a subtype of the psychotic. Frequently the differential diagnosis between the borderline personality and schizophrenia presents little difficulty. The differential diagnosis here focuses primarily on reality testing and thought processes. The schizophrenic individual is one who either constantly demonstrates distortions in reality testing and/or thought processes, or at best must use a continuous expenditure of energy to prevent these distortions from surfacing. Schizophrenia, however, has been defined and diagnosed in a wide variety of ways. The differential diagnosis between the borderline personality and schizophrenia depends on how the two terms are defined. Chapter 13 will be devoted to exploring the different definitions and diagnostic systems for schizophrenia.

The Borderline Personality and Depression

Recently much focus has been placed on the differential diagnosis between the borderline personality and depression. Donald Klein (1977) views many borderline patients as representing a subgroup of the affective disorders. Klein has described a number of specific syndromes (hysteroid dysphoria, emotionally unstable character disorder, phobic anxiety reactions, and others) that basically fall within the borderline group by other classifications. He has sought to demonstrate that these syndromes are actually subgroups of affective disorders and respond to various antidepressants. Klein believes that the psychic structure of the borderline patient has been overemphasized and that too little attention has been paid to the patient's longitudinal affective status.

It is possible that a subgroup of borderline individuals overlaps diagnostically with depressives, in that this subgroup is vulnerable to depressions and can suffer superimposed depressions. This subgroup should not necessarily be diagnosed as depressed, however. Rather, these people can be viewed as individuals with borderline psychic organizations who in addition suffer superimposed depressions. Analogously, individuals with neurotic or psychotic psychic organizations can also suffer superimposed depressions. There is some research (Stone 1977, Akiskal 1981, Pope, Jonas, Hudson, et al. 1983) supporting an overlap of the borderline personality with depression. It seems likely that such individuals demonstrate both disorders simultaneously, however, rather than that the borderline is a subgroup of the affective disorders.

The Borderline Personality and Organicity

Organicity is typically associated with the global defects of disorientation, loss of recent memory, and impairment in intellectual functioning. In addition there are often numerous more subtle defects, such as impaired judgment, a labile and shallow affect, concrete thinking, irritability, and decreased frustration tolerance and impulse control. Because the global defects basically do not occur in the borderline individual, there should be no problems in differential diagnosis when these impairments are apparent. Problems are encountered with organic states that are not associated with any of the more global organic defects. Such states include those following ingestion of various drugs, such as phencyclidine hydrochloride (PCP). In these instances there are sometimes specific subtle signs and symptoms corresponding to the various ingested substances. These signs and symptoms, in conjunction with a careful history taking and appropriate laboratory tests, should be helpful in formulating the differential diagnosis. Andrulonis, Gloeck, Stroebel, and co-workers (1981) indicate that some borderline individuals may overlap diagnostically with patients in several distinct organic subgroups, including an episodic dyscontrol group and a minimal brain dysfunction group. There may well be a subgroup of borderline patients related to these organic impairments.

The Borderline Personality and Adolescence

The adolescent "normally" experiences a number of problems similar to those of the borderline individual. These include problems of identity, rapidly shifting defensive patterns, problems with frustration tolerance and impulse control, and affective instability. In the adolescent neither defensive patterns nor a well-defined and integrated sense of self (and objects) has yet coalesced. When attempting to make the diagnosis of borderline personality in adolescence, the same ego psychological diagnostic approach that has been outlined for adults applies. However, before the consolidation of both defensive functioning and identity formation, the diagnosis of borderline personality should be made only with the utmost scrutiny and caution.

CHAPTER 12

The Narcissistic Personality

Like the borderline personality, the narcissistic personality made its first appearance in the official psychiatric nomenclature with *DSM-III* (American Psychiatric Association 1980). The popularity of the term stems from the emergence and preeminence of the extensive writings of Kohut (1966, 1968, 1971, 1972, 1977; Kohut and Wolf 1978) and Kernberg (1970, 1974, 1975, 1976a, 1980a). Current concepts of the narcissistic personality, including those of *DSM-III*, are based almost exclusively on their works. Despite several excellent publications (Rothstein 1979, Akhtar and Thomson 1982) offering clarification, there still is confusion regarding the term *narcissistic personality*. This chapter, taken in part from another publication (Goldstein, 1985a), will first attempt to arrive at a better understanding of the term.

The Work of Kohut

Working predominantly within the framework of clinical psychoanalysis, Kohut (1966, 1968, 1971, 1972, 1977; Kohut and Wolf 1978) emphasizes the spontaneous emergence during

123

the course of analysis of one of several elaborately described narcissistic transferences, or a combination of these. Such transferences are most critical for making the definitive diagnosis of narcissistic personality. Emphasis is placed on allowing these transferences to emerge spontaneously, without interference by early interpretation.

The two transferences extensively described are the mirror transference and the idealizing transference. In the mirror transference an early need for parental accepting, conforming, or mirroring is revived in the treatment situation. In the idealizing transference an early need for merging with an idealized parent is analogously revived in the treatment situation. The emergence of these transferences reflects current pathological narcissistic configurations originating in the earliest times of life secondary to severe absence of various appropriate and empathic responses by the parents. The details of these various transferences and narcissistic configurations, thought to be indicative of the patient's core psychopathology, are elaborated by Kohut and his co-workers.

Although these narcissistic configurations arise from developmental deficiencies from an earlier period and are thus primitive and archaic, they are stable and cohesive and basically resist disruptive fragmentation. To Kohut, this stability is crucial, because it is the characteristic that distinguishes these narcissistic configurations from the more pathological borderline configurations and that enables the narcissistic patient, unlike the borderline, to undergo psychoanalysis. In contrast to the narcissistic personality, the borderline patient has a very unstable sense of self, subject to easy fragmentation and regression. Kernberg's concept of identity diffusion (1975, 1977, 1980a, 1980b, 1981) as being characteristic of the borderline patient complements Kohut's theory here.

One definition of psychoanalysis demands that the pathogenic nucleus of the analysand's personality become activated in the treatment situation and enter into a specific transference with the analyst, a transference that is gradually worked through in the analytic process by analytic interventions alone. Because of the cohesion and stability of the narcissistic configurations, Kohut maintains that this process can take place in the case of the narcissistic personality. In contrast, because of the underlying unstable sense of self and identity diffusion in the borderline patient, psychoanalysis there produces disruptive fragmentation and regression. Thus Kohut groups the borderline individual with the psychotic as being unanalyzable, and distinguishes these patients from the analyzable narcissistic personality. The fact that there are fleeting regressions in response to slights and rebuffs during the course of analysis in the narcissistic personality, indicative of the syndrome of narcissistic vulnerability (to be discussed later), does not take away from the cohesiveness and stability of these analyzable patients.

To help explain the origins of the pathological narcissistic configurations, Kohut initially amended classical psychoanalytic theory by hypothesizing the existence of a new and separate line of development. This narcissistic line of development was posited to stand alongside the libidinal and the aggressive lines of development. Kohut viewed the pathological narcissistic configurations as arising from lacks in development along this narcissistic developmental line, lacks that could arise anywhere from birth through latency. He further postulated the establishment early in life of two normally occurring configurations along the narcissistic line of development, the grandiose self and the idealized parent imago. These narcissistic configurations relate to the mirror and idealizing transferences, respectively. In the course of normal development, under favorable conditions, these normally occurring narcissistic configurations become integrated into the rest of the personality. The grandiosity and exhibitionism of the grandiose self eventually supply the syntonic ambitions and purposes, contribute to enjoyment in activities, and are instrumental in the building of self-esteem. The idealized parent imago eventually becomes internalized as the idealized superego and provides one's ideals and guidelines. If the child suffers severe parental neglect, reflected in the absence of various appropriate and empathic responses related to either of these normally occurring narcissistic configurations, then these configurations do not become integrated into the rest of the personality. Instead, they remain as archaic configurations, constituting the core of the narcissistic personality. The exact nature of the pathological narcissistic configuration will correspond to the timing and the severity of the parental pathological responses, and to the extent of the involvement of the two normally occurring narcissistic configurations.

Later, Kohut (1977) abandoned the model of a third and separate developmental line as critical to the understanding of the narcissistic personality, conceptualizing narcissistic psychopathology in terms of miscarriages in the normal development of the self in response to self objects. The self became the center of analytic study; developmental lines became seen as constituents of the self. Despite this change in emphasis, the original theory of a separate narcissistic line of development remains very useful in helping one understand Kohut's conception of narcissistic personality. The "classical" psychoanalysts do not accept either Kohut's original or his revised theories, believing that the narcissistic personality can be adequately explained without any theoretical innovations.

KOHUT ON A DESCRIPTIVE LEVEL

As noted, Kohut relies on the spontaneous emergence of a specific transference during psychoanalysis to establish the diagnosis of narcissistic personality. He does speak, however, of descriptive features that can be useful in alerting one to the possibility of narcissistic psychopathology during evaluation interviews. Kohut cautions against using these descriptive features to make the definitive diagnosis. The descriptive features can be divided into four groups. The first is a tendency for symptoms to be vague and ill defined. The patient is unclear about why he is seeking help, and the therapist often has to ask specific questions to attain clarity here. Sometimes secondary complaints, such as work inhibitions or sexual problems, are described, but the chief complaints remain elusive.

The second descriptive feature is the syndrome of narcissistic vulnerability. Narcissistic patients have highly labile self-esteems. These patients are exceedingly sensitive to slights, rejections, rebuffs, disappointments, and failures. Reactions to slights or perceived slights are commonly seen in the therapeutic situation but are also noted with regard to significant relationships outside the therapeutic setting. The slights, no matter how subtle, often produce very uncomfortable feelings, along with disruptive behavior. The patient may become bored or depressed, feel dull and empty, begin to do his work without vigor or zest, lose his initiative, begin to brood, or become preoccupied with his body. Compensatory defenses against these feelings, such as various kinds of stimulating and dangerous acting-out behavior, perverse sexuality, and drug and alcohol overuse, may ensue. With the undoing of the slight, or with praise or admiration, the uncomfortable feelings and disruptive behavior stop, and the patient can again begin to feel alive and happy and to regain his initiative. To this pronounced sensitivity to slights and rejections, with the corresponding onset of very uncomfortable feelings and disruptive behavior, is assigned the name *narcissistic vulnerability*. It is a core problem in the narcissistic personality and presents itself again and again over the course of therapy.

The third descriptive feature is the occurrence of specific pathological feeling states. The feeling states of grandiosity, uncomfortable excitement, embarrassment, shame, humiliation, and narcissistic rage are clearly associated with the narcissistic personality. They stand in contrast to the typical feeling states associated with the neurotic patient, (castration) anxiety and guilt. These pathological feeling states often occur in response to perceived slights, rebuffs, and rejections and thus are clearly related to the syndrome of narcissistic vulnerability. They represent even more uncomfortable and pathological feelings than those described in the last paragraph. Exquisitely painful, these pathological feeling states also are very often defended against by stimulating and dangerous acting-out behavior, perverse sexuality, and drug and alcohol overuse. Believing that true drug addicts constitute a subgroup of the narcissistic personality, Wurmser (1974) describes how drugs are regularly used as an artificial defense against these overwhelming feeling states in these patients. He goes on to correlate the use of specific drugs with the occurence of specific pathological feeling states.

The feeling state most frequently written about, extensively by Kohut (1972), is narcissistic rage. Here a slight, rejection, or rebuff is felt as a severe attack on the self. The hurt, humiliation, and embarrassment of the slight are so deeply felt that the individual responds either with shameful withdrawal or with narcissistic rage. The rage is usually expressed directly, may be accompanied by frenzied action, and often includes the desire and need for revenge, as a way of undoing the hurt. Sometimes the revenge is pursued compulsively and relentlessly without regard for reality, because the attacker is seen as an inhuman, depersonified enemy. The term *narcissistic rage* is actually used to describe a wide spectrum of feelings, always in response to slights. This wide spectrum can be viewed as a continuum, with reactions such as mild annoyance or fleeting anger at one end, and more severe reactions, such as murderous rage or life-long vengeful attempts at retaliation, at the other.

The last of Kohut's descriptive features consists of the symptom complexes. Some of these have already been mentioned and discussed.

1. *Sexuality*: perverse fantasies and lack of sexual interest
2. *Social relations*: work inhibitions, inability to form and maintain significant relationships, delinquent activities
3. *Manifest personality*: lack of humor, empathy, and sense of proportion; tendency toward rage reactions, pathological lying
4. *Psychosomatic sphere*: hypochondriacal preoccupations

The Work of Kernberg

Like Kohut's, Kernberg's work (1970, 1974, 1975, 1976a, 1980a) lies predominantly within the framework of clinical psychoanalysis. Theoretically, Kernberg is in disagreement with Kohut. Kernberg sees no need for either the concept of a separate narcissistic line of development or a conceptual framework focusing on the centrality of the self. Rather, he believes that the narcissistic personality can be adequately explained without any theoretical innovations. He views the narcissistic personality as the outcome of the early development of very specific *psychopathological* structures rather than the result of the lack of development of normal narcissistic configurations. He focuses on the aggressive drive as playing a causative role in the narcissistic personality and criticizes Kohut for neglecting this mechanism. Unlike Kohut, who clearly differentiates the narcissistic personality from the borderline, Kernberg believes that many narcissistic patients fit into the borderline group. Kernberg also differs from Kohut in recommending a wider range of treatment approaches, corresponding to the variations in psychopathology seen within the narcissistic group.

In contrast to Kohut, Kernberg supplies much detail in descriptive features in his writings. Despite his theoretical differences with Kohut, Kernberg's descriptions of the narcissistic personality are somewhat similar to those of Kohut. Kernberg describes the narcissistic personality as the extreme in the pathological development of narcissism. He sees these patients as expressively absorbed in themselves and as having distortions in their internal relationships with other people. They are grandiose and extremely self-centered and display an absence of interest and empathy in others, except in reference to themselves. There is a curious contradiction in that these patients have very inflated and grandiose concepts of themselves, yet they display an inordinate need for praise and tribute from others to maintain these concepts. They search for gratifications confirming their grandiosity, and sometimes show conscious feelings of inferiority and insecurity alternating with the feelings of grandiosity and omnipotence. They receive little gratification in life outside of praise and tributes and their own grandiose fantasies, and can sometimes feel bored, empty, and restless. Kernberg goes on to describe even more pathological aspects of the narcissistic personality: the tendency to envy others; the tendency to idealize those from whom they expect narcissistic supplies while devaluating those from whom they expect nothing; their exploitative and parasitic relationships; their sense of entitlement; the coldness and ruthlessness behind their often superficial charm; their lack of emotional depth and failure to understand the emotions of others; their inability to experience true depression.

Kernberg believes that severe "structural" psychopathology

lies behind these descriptive characteristics, related to very early primitive, internalized object relations. He stresses the active development of these pathological structures early in life. These pathological structures are characterized by the pathological fusion of the ideal self, the ideal object, and the actual self. Underlying these structures are often paranoid traits related to the projection of early rage. These structures are thought to develop in an early atmosphere created by chronically cold parents, with covert but intense aggression. Using an elaboration of these formulations, Kernberg is able to explain the dynamics and descriptive characteristics of the narcissistic personality.

The Narcissistic Personality and the Borderline

An important question addressed by Kernberg is whether the narcissistic personality fits into the borderline group. To address this question, we will again be making comparisons with the four relative ego strengths and four ego weaknesses described in the ego psychological diagnostic approach to the borderline personality. The most striking difference in comparing Kernberg's narcissistic personality with the borderline is in the area of identity diffusion. Instead of an unintegrated and unstable identity, the narcissistic personality has an integrated, although highly pathological, identity based on a grandiose self. Underlying this identity is a fusion of the ideal self, the ideal object, and the actual self. We should note at this point that Kernberg divides narcissistic personalities into three groups. One group, despite the narcissistic identity, by definition functions on an overtly borderline level. In the other two groups, the integrated, although highly pathological, identity helps bring about a greater stability than in the typical borderline individual. For the sake of clarity, these latter two groups will be classified together and termed Kernberg's "healthier" narcissistic personalities. This "healthier" group evidences better adaptation to reality, less difficulty with impulse control and frustration tolerance, and less affective instability than the borderline individual. Reality testing, thought processes, and interpersonal relations are all maintained more effectively. The defensive organization of this group remains primitive, with a predominance of splitting, denial, projection, omnipotence, and primitive idealization. Kernberg recommends psycho-analysis for these "healthier" narcissistic personalities, in clear contrast to the group functioning overtly on a borderline level. He does not indicate clearly whether this "healthier" group fits into the borderline category. When viewed in accordance with the ego psychological diagnostic approach, this "healthier" group, although having some definite similarities to the border-line personality, basically does not fulfill the criteria for that diagnosis.

If we compare Kernberg's "healthier" narcissistic group with Kohut's narcissistic personality, we find a striking sim-ilarity. In a manner analogous to Kernberg's, Kohut sees his narcissistic personality as having a stable and cohesive, al-though primitive and archaic, identity, an identity in marked contrast to that of identity diffusion. We can again focus on the ego psychological diagnostic approach, this time with regard to Kohut's narcissistic personality. We find that reality testing, impulse control and frustration tolerance, and stability of affects are all relatively stronger in the narcissistic personality than in the borderline. As in the borderline personality, these functions are sensitive to regression. In the borderline per-sonality, however, these functions are more globally sensitive; in the narcissistic personality this sensitivity is limited to the area of narcissistic vulnerability. Interpersonal relations, very intact superficially, are maintained to a better degree than in the borderline individual yet are still distorted by narcissistic configurations. Adaptation to reality is better than in the borderline individual, and thought processes remain intact. Defenses, under the influence of the narcissistic configur-ations, include primitive idealization, omnipotence, devalua-tion, and splitting, a group very similar to that described by Kernberg.

Like Kernberg's "healthier" narcissistic group, Kohut's narcissistic personality, when evaluated according to the ego psychological diagnostic approach, does not meet the di-agnostic criteria for the borderline personality. Instead, this group, like Kernberg's "healthier" group, seems to stand in between the borderline and the neurotic states in degree of psychopathology. Kernberg (1976a, 1977, 1980b, 1981) has offered a conceptual framework in which he classifies all patients as demonstrating one of three levels of psychic functioning. These levels of psychic functioning, all characterized by underlying distinct structural configurations, include the neurotic, the borderline, and the psychotic. Given the preceding discussion of Kohut's narcissistic personality and Kernberg's "healthier" narcissistic personality, a fourth level of psychic functioning can possibly be added to Kernberg's conceptualization. This level, the narcissistic level, also with a distinct underlying structural configuration, falls between the neurotic and the borderline in the degree of psychopathology.

DSM-III

With the coming of *DSM-III* (American Psychiatric Association 1980), the narcissistic personality for the first time has been included in the official psychiatric nomenclature. In *DSM-III* the primary focus is on symptoms and traits, ideally those that can differentiate the narcissistic personality from other patient groups. Typically in this approach, literature reviews, research designs, and statistical methods are employed to try to identify these traits and symptoms. In the case of the *DSM-III* diagnosis of the borderline personality, much preliminary work of this nature was undertaken.

In the case of the narcissistic personality, however, preliminary work of this nature has been minimal. There have been virtually no studies establishing the reliability or validity of the conceptualization of the narcissistic personality. The literature review, judging from the end results of *DSM-III*, seems to have been confined to the work of Kohut and Kernberg. The research-oriented group would be the first to criticize the *DSM-III* criteria for the diagnosis of the narcissistic personality on this basis. Yet the *DSM-III* criteria do seem to describe a distinct group of patients, frequently seen in private practice.

To make the diagnosis of narcissistic personality according to *DSM-III*, the following five traits must be characteristic of the individual's current and long-term functioning:

A. Grandiose sense of self-importance or uniqueness, e.g., exaggeration of achievements and talents, focus on the special nature of one's problems.
B. Preoccupation with fantasies of unlimited success, power, brilliance, beauty, or ideal love.
C. Exhibitionism: the person requires constant attention and admiration.
D. Cool indifference or marked feelings of rage, inferiority, shame, humiliation, or emptiness in response to criticism, indifference of others, or defeat....
E. At least two of the following are characteristic of disturbances in interpersonal relationships:
    1) entitlement: expectation of special favors without assuming reciprocal responsibilities; e.g., surprise and anger that people will not do what is wanted;
    2) interpersonal exploitativeness: taking advantage of others to indulge own desires or for self-aggrandizement; disregard for the personal integrity and rights of others;
    3) relationships that characteristically alternate between the extremes of overidealization and devaluation;
    4) lack of empathy: inability to recognize how others feel; e.g., unable to appreciate the distress of someone who is seriously ill.

DSM-III AND KOHUT

Using this same symptom-oriented checklist approach, one can take either Kohut's or Kernberg's descriptive aspects of the narcissistic personality and recast them in accordance with this model. Although this application would probably be viewed quite negatively by Kohut, and possibly by Kernberg also, it should prove useful in comparing Kohut's and Kernberg's ideas with those expressed in *DSM-III*.

When we apply this method to Kohut's work, we find that a diagnosis of narcissistic personality is predicated on the following characteristics of the individual's current and long-term functioning:

1. Chief complaints that are vague and ill defined
2. The syndrome of narcissistic vulnerability (the pronounced

sensitivity to slights and rejections, plus the corresponding
tendency to respond to these slights and rejections with very
uncomfortable feelings and very disruptive behavior)
3. The proclivity to experiencing certain pathological feelings
   states: grandiosity, excitement, embarrassment, humiliation,
   shame, hypochondriasis, and narcissistic rage
4. At least one of the following symptom complexes:
   a. *Sexuality*: perverse fantasies or lack of sexual interest
   b. *Social relations*: work inhibitions, inability to form and
      maintain significant relationships; delinquent activities
   c. *Manifest personality*: lack of humor, empathy, sense of
      proportion; tendency to rage reactions, pathological
      lying
   d. *Psychosomatic sphere*: hypochondriacal preoccupations

DSM-III AND KERNBERG

When we apply this method to Kernberg's work, we find that a
diagnosis of narcissistic personality hinges on the existence of
the following characteristics of the individual's current and
long-term functioning:

1. Grandiosity and extreme self-centeredness
2. The curious contradiction of having a very inflated and
   grandiose concept of oneself, and simultaneously an inordinate need for praise and tribute from others to maintain
   this concept
3. An absence of interest and empathy in others, except to
   confirm one's self image
4. At least four of the following features:
   a. A search for gratifications confirming one's grandiosity
   b. Enjoyment in life lacking except from praise from others,
      plus one's own grandiose fantasies
   c. Vulnerability to bored, restless, and uncomfortable states
      when one does not receive tribute and praise
   d. Pathological envy
   e. Idealization of those who give narcissistic supplies, and
      devaluation of those who do not
   f. Exploitative and parasitic relationships
   g. Sense of entitlement

h. Coldness and ruthlessness, often behind a superficial charm

i. Alternation of feelings of inferiority and insecurity with those of grandiosity and omnipotence.

CONCLUSIONS REGARDING *DSM-III*

All the *DSM-III* diagnostic criteria for the narcissistic personality are derived from the work of either Kohut or Kernberg. Criterion a of the *DSM-III* criteria corresponds directly to criterion 1 of Kernberg. *DSM-III* criterion B, possibly somewhat redundant in respect to *DSM-III* criterion A, corresponds directly to 1, 4a, and 4b of Kernberg. *DSM-III* criterion C corresponds to 2 of Kohut and 2, 4b, and 4c of Kernberg. *DSM-III* criterion D corresponds to 2 and 3 of Kohut and 4c of Kernberg. *DSM-III* criterion E1 corresponds to 4g of Kernberg. *DSM-III* criterion E2 corresponds to 4f of Kernberg. *DSM-III* criterion E3 corresponds to 4e of Kernberg. *DSM-III* criterion E4 corresponds to 3 of Kernberg and 3c of Kohut.

Of Kohut's criteria, 2 and 3 appear to be of most importance. Of Kernberg's criteria, 1, 2, and 3 seem most critical. The *DSM-III* criteria clearly capture these most important criteria of both Kohut and Kernberg. In addition, *DSM-III* includes several other criteria, primarily of Kernberg. One can object to the overlap of *DSM-III* criteria A and B, to the use of the term *exhibitionism* in criterion C, to the choice of the pathological feelings cited in D, and to the selective inclusion of items 1 to 4 in E in preference to other important items from the conceptualizations of Kohut and Kernberg. Of greater importance, one can criticize *DSM-III* for failing to portray the sense of contradiction so clearly apparent in the narcissistic personality, exemplified best by Kernberg's criterion 2, and for failing to provide dynamic linkages among the various criteria. These criticisms, however, are not of major importance. The *DSM-III* criteria do represent, in a clearly defined way, a descriptive compilation of the works of Kohut and Kernberg. They also describe a distinct group of patients frequently appearing in the offices of mental health professionals, and thus seem clearly useful in the clinical setting.

CHAPTER 13

Schizophrenia

This chapter explores the different influential systems of the twentieth century regarding the diagnosis of schizophrenia. A clarification of "schizophrenia" will concomitantly clarify the differential diagnosis of borderline and schizophrenic conditions. Parts of this chapter are related to several previous publications (Goldstein 1979, 1983)

Kraepelin

Any current attempt to look at the definition and the diagnosis of schizophrenia must begin with Kraepelin (1896). Kraepelin's main work began in the 1890s. At that time he differentiated the condition denoted by *dementia praecox*, the precursor to the term *schizophrenia*, from other psychoses. Dementia praecox had an early onset and a downhill course leading to intellectual deterioration. Symptoms were thought to include hallucinations, delusions, disorders of thought, changes in speech consequent to the disorders of thought, lack of insight and judgment, flattening of affect, negativism, stereotypes, and decreased attention to the outer world. Kraepelin came upon his richly elaborated descriptions by repeated observation and did not utilize any underlying conceptual framework. His greatest contribution is probably these detailed descriptions, yet he is possibly best known for his concept of dementia praecox as a disease process of early onset with a gradual but inexorable downhill course. There is some question about whether Kraepelin actually thought of dementia praecox as always having such characteristics (Sartorius 1973), yet a Kraepelinian concept of schizophrenia in this country became synonymous with early onset, downhill course, and poor prognosis. As a result, in the 1900s, when much zeal was associated with positive therapeutic approaches to schizophrenic patients, the Kraepelinian concept came into disfavor. It remained poorly regarded until its reemergence in the Feighner criteria for schizophrenia (Feighner, Robins, Guze, et al. 1972), and then in *DSM-III* (1980).

Bleuler and the Four As

Eugen Bleuler has demonstrated more influence on the diagnosis of schizophrenia than any other twentieth-century figure in this country. Unlike Kraepelin, Bleuler (1950) did not believe that schizophrenia necessarily had a poor prognosis or an inevitable downhill course. In 1911 he created the term *schizophrenia* and defined the term on the basis of specific underlying processes. He divided the symptoms of schizophrenia into two groups, fundamental and accessory. Fundamental symptoms were those thought to be indicative of the specific underlying processes and thus were pathognomonic. Accessory symptoms, although frequently present, were neither specific for schizophrenia nor diagnostic. The accessory symptoms included those phenomena associated with any psychoses, such as delusions and hallucinations. The fundamental symptoms constituted what have come to be known as Bleuler's four As:

1. Defect in *association* (characterized by loosening of associations and by other evidence of a thinking disturbance)

2. Defect in *affect* (characterized by flat or blunted affect or affect inappropriate to the ideation or situation)
3. *Autism* (characterized by a detachment from external reality and a proclivity to withdraw into one's fantasies and inner life)
4. *Ambivalence* (characterized by the existence of opposite feelings and thoughts simultaneously)

Using Bleuler's approach, the diagnosis of schizophrenia was made if the patient exhibited these four *A*s (or some of them). Determining the existence of ambivalence (demonstrating true schizophrenic ambivalence and differentiating it from other forms of ambivalence) has proved to be very difficult. Therefore, many have eliminated this *A* when using Bleuler's system for diagnosing schizophrenia. Of the four *A*s, Bleuler attributed primary importance to the defect in association. Following his lead, many have focused on this one defect itself as being pathognomonic for the diagnosis of schizophrenia. Thus, schizophrenia has been considered by many to be a disorder of thinking (as opposed especially to a disorder of mood). Corresponding to the focus on schizophrenia as a thinking disorder was the tendency by some to try to demonstrate formal thought disorders and to make the diagnosis of schizophrenia on this basis. To some the demonstration of a thought disorder has been the sine qua non for the diagnosis of schizophrenia.

The Ego in Schizophrenia

Another major influence on the diagnosis of schizophrenia in American psychiatry in the twentieth century has come from ego psychology. Schizophrenia is conceptualized as an ego "disease," and the schizophrenic is characterized by his or her ego deficit or ego weakness. If the ego can be measured by its functions, then the schizophrenic can be expected to demonstrate obvious weaknesses in the various ego functions. Thus, in a way analogous to the ego psychological diagnostic approach to the borderline personality, an ego profile for the schizophrenic can be compiled by focusing on the ego functions, as originally described by Bellak (1958, 1970) and Beres (1956).

FUNCTIONS RELATING TO REALITY

Adaptation to reality.   In acute states the difficulty in this function is often so severe that the patient is unable to function outside a structured situation, such as a hospital. Severe difficulties in adapting to the external world result from such symptoms as confusion, upsurges of aggression, misinterpretations, delusions, hallucinations, and various fears. In chronic states impairment varies markedly. At one extreme is the person who is full of incapacitating symptoms and is unable to cope in the external world; at the other extreme is the individual with few symptoms who has learned to live with these symptoms to the extent that they do not interfere with her daily life.

Reality testing.   There are always some defects in reality testing, both in acute and in chronic states. In acute states these are often obvious and global. In chronic states they can range from the extreme of being obvious and global (as in acute states) to the extreme of being operative only in selected areas of functioning. In some cases a patient will be able to ignore or isolate her defects in reality testing and to adapt to reality quite well. For example, a delusional patient may ignore her delusions. The schizophrenic shows major impairment in reality testing, constantly demonstrating some distortions in this area or relying on a continuous expenditure of energy to prevent these reality distortions from surfacing.

Sense of reality.   There will frequently be defects in the sense of reality, in both acute and chronic states. These can be fleeting, occurring at times of stress, or can recur continually. Examples of such defects include confused body images, feelings of estrangement, derealization, and depersonalization.

Although closely related to reality testing, subtle defects in the sense of reality can occur without obvious disturbances in reality testing.

IMPULSE CONTROL AND FRUSTRATION TOLERANCE

The schizophrenic shows frequent disturbances in this area, often characterized by outbreaks of aggression or by extreme defenses against this (such as catatonia). Some have theorized that one of the central difficulties in schizophrenia is the inability of the patient to handle his aggression. Thus, M. Klein (Segal 1964) has hypothesized that the main defect in schizophrenia is too much death instinct. Bak (1954) has stated that the ego's inability to neutralize the aggressive drives constitutes the core problem in schizophrenia, and Hartmann (1953) has also related schizophrenia to the inability of the ego to neutralize aggression.

Difficulties with the sexual (or libidinal) drive are also encountered in schizophrenia. Freud (1911, 1914) based his theory of schizophrenia on this notion. He particularly emphasized the relationship of unconscious homosexual impulses to the outbreak of delusions of persecution; this relationship is frequently evident clinically. Although Freud emphasized the exclusiveness of this relationship, today we can postulate an upsurge of either the libidinal (heterosexual or homosexual) or of the aggressive drive as playing a key role in psychotic symptom formation.

THOUGHT PROCESSES

In the Bleulerian system the presence of a thought disorder is considered pathognomonic for schizophrenia. Recent psychiatric research (Pope and Lipinski 1978, Pope, Lipinski, Cohen, et al. 1980, Procci 1976), however, has questioned this exclusive relationship. Although not necessarily pathognomonic, marked or frequent problems in conceptual thinking are frequently associated with schizophrenia. When present, these problems vary in presentation, sometimes being overtly obvious and sometimes demonstrable only on psychological tests.

INTERPERSONAL RELATIONS

There are usually defects in interpersonal relations in the schizophrenic. Defects range from subtle to obvious and show considerable variability among patients. Thus, on the one hand there are schizophrenics with obvious and diffuse defects in this area, and on the other there are those who are able to maintain adequate interpersonal relations, at least on a superficial level. Typical disturbances include symbiotic, narcissistic, and even autistic forms of relating. There is a common tendency to use another person simply to meet one's own needs, or even to distort one's object representation of another to "make" the individual more in accordance with one's own needs. The schizophrenic may tend to stay aloof, withdrawn, and to himself, or, alternately, to form clinging, demanding, and intense relationships with others.

SELF AND OBJECT REPRESENTATIONS

Although the term *identity diffusion* is most commonly applied to the borderline patient, it also is applicable to the schizophrenic. The schizophrenic is lacking in a concept of self and objects. He retains multiple, unintegrated, vacillating, and sometimes fragmented concepts of himself and others. Different images are invoked at different times, sometimes in rapid succession. A comprehensive image of the self (and objects) is never integrated in a meaningful way, as identity is lacking. In addition to these problems, the schizophrenic is characterized by a more severe difficulty, that of fusion of self and object images. When these fusions occur, they lead to corresponding blurring of reality.

DEFENSES

Although there is much variation in the use of defenses, there is a definite tendency in the schizophrenic toward the use of more primitive defenses. The typical schizophrenic uses a combination of neurotic, immature, borderline, and narcissistic defenses in day-to-day functioning and has a tendency to use narcissistic defenses under stress. Typically, projection and denial are among those defenses frequently used in day-to-day functioning. The narcissistic defenses characteristic of the schizophrenic include delusions, hallucinations, fusion, fragmentation, and dedifferentiation. There is commonly a defect in repression, and for this reason the schizophrenic will often seem more in contact with feelings and thoughts that most people are not aware of in themselves. As a result, there will sometimes be the tendency for the patient to talk openly about subjects usually censored by others, such as incestuous and murderous feelings.

Although this ego psychological approach emphasizes ego weaknesses, an ego evaluation also permits one to note ego strengths. Thus, the examination of the ego functions in any given patient, by yielding an inventory of strengths and weaknesses, can provide an excellent framework not only for diagnosis, but also for prognosis, psychodynamic understanding, and therapeutic planning.

Schneider's First-Rank Symptoms

Another approach to the diagnosis of schizophrenia, employed in Europe in the mid-twentieth century but relatively neglected in this country until recently, is Schneider's conceptualization of first-rank symptoms of schizophrenia (1959). According to Schneider, any one of eight symptoms is pathognomonic for schizophrenia.

1. *Auditorization of thought* (the patient's hearing his own thoughts)
2. *Auditory hallucinations* that occur in a form of running commentary on the patient's current thoughts and activities

or that are experienced in the form of a conversation between two or more people who refer to the patient in the third person

3. *Thought withdrawal*
4. *Thought insertion*
5. *Thought broadcasting*
6. *Somatic hallucinations* that the patient attributes to the will, influence, or motive of outside agencies
7. *Delusional perceptions* (delusions based on perceptions—for example, seeing a cow move its head means that the patient had better go home and change his shirt)
8. *Events in the sphere of feeling, drive, and volition that are experienced as made or influenced by others*

A number of Schneider's first-rank symptoms (3, 4, 5, 6, 8, and possibly 7) can easily be perceived to be related to Mahler's developmental theories concerning schizophrenia (1970). The feeling of being influenced and controlled by others can be seen to be directly related to problems of the symbiotic period, when the child is influenced and controlled by the mother and has difficulty differentiating himself from her. Schneider's symptoms are also closely related to Federn's concept of schizophrenia as being primarily related to defective ego boundaries (1952). Despite these relationships, Schneider's system is atheoretical and based exclusively on clinical experiences with patients.

Broad vs. Narrow Diagnostic Concepts of Schizophrenia

The diagnostic systems reviewed thus far vary in the numbers of patients that each diagnose as schizophrenic. The Kraepelinian and Schneiderian systems, most prevalent in Europe, include relatively few patients and thus offer a narrow definition of schizophrenia. The Bleulerian system and ego function approach, most prevalent in the United States, include many more patients and offer a broad definition of schizophrenia.

This difference in narrow vs. broad definitions was clearly demonstrated in a study comparing American and British diagnoses of schizophrenia through the United States -United

Kingdom Gross National Project in 1972 (Cooper, Kendell, Gurland, et al. 1972). As a part of this study, patients in New York hospitals were diagnosed by the New York staff and compared with patients in London hospitals, diagnosed by the London staff. The rate of the diagnosis of schizophrenia by the New York staff was double the rate of the London staff. When the project staff, using their own criteria, compared the same New York and London samples, however, their rates of diagnosing schizophrenia were basically equal in the two groups. This study highlighted the differences in diagnosis between New York and London (and probably between the United States and Europe) in 1972. It also highlighted the differences between the broad and narrow diagnostic approaches to schizophrenia.

Recently Devised Diagnostic Systems

A number of diagnostic systems for schizophrenia have been devised recently in this country. These exhibit several trends here. One is to bridge the gap between the broad and narrow definitions, basically by providing narrower approaches. Another is to provide a diagnostic system that can be used readily for research purposes, one that can allow for descriptive diagnoses that are easily determined, reliable, and valid. Elaborate statistical methods and massive samples of patients have been employed to find those symptoms that are most diagnostic of schizophrenia. Another trend has been to include longitudinal criteria within the diagnostic system. Thus, clinical course and duration of illness have come to play a role in some of these newer classifications. In sum, the newer systems have tended to give a narrow definition, to be research and description oriented, to look for reliability and validity, and to include the longitudinal factor of clinical course.

The newer diagnostic systems include the New Haven Schizophrenic Index (Astrachan, Harrow, Adler, et al. 1972), Carpenter and Strauss's Flexible System for the Diagnosis of Schizophrenia (1973), the Feighner criteria of the Washington University group (Feighner, Robins, Guze, et al. 1972), and the

Research Diagnostic Criteria of Spitzer, Endicott, and Robins (1978). These four diagnostic systems have been described and compared, along with Schneider's first-rank symptoms and *DSM-III*, in a recent article by Fenton, Mosher, and Matthews (1981).

The New Haven group, in developing the New Haven Schizophrenic Index (Astrachan, Harrow, Adler, et al. 1972), used a large sample and statistical methods to attempt to establish those symptoms most clearly associated with schizophrenia. A list of symptoms in six different categories was constructed, and a system was established whereby symptoms were given certain numbers of points. The symptoms included various delusions and hallucinations, various kinds of thinking disturbances, inappropriate affect, paranoid ideation, confusion, and various kinds of catatonic behavior. A total of four points was necessary to establish the diagnosis of schizophrenia.

The Flexible System for Diagnosis of Schizophrenia (Carpenter and Strauss 1973) was another attempt using a large sample and statistical methods to establish empirically those symptoms most clearly associated with schizophrenia. Here, twelve symptoms were established that were highly correlated with schizophrenia: restricted affect, poor insight, thoughts aloud, poor rapport, widespread delusions, incoherent speech, unreliable information, bizzare delusions, nihilistic delusions, the absence of early awakening, the absence of depressed facies, and the absence of elation. Statistical tables were devised to indicate how many of these symptoms would be optimal to best discriminate schizophrenia from other diagnostic entities. The authors concluded that five or six symptoms would be the most useful criterion for the diagnosis of schizophrenia.

The Feighner group (Feighner, Robins, Guze, et al. 1972) posited that schizophrenic conditions with good and poor prognoses were two different disease entities. Holding that the poor-prognosis schizophrenics were the "true" schizophrenics, they established diagnostic criteria that would distinguish this group. By including the longitudinal factors of duration of illness and poor premorbid adjustment in the diagnostic criteria, they reintroduced Kraepelinian concepts into American psychiatry. According to this system, the patient must meet three criteria. First, she has to have the "illness" for at least six consecutive months. Second, the illness must be characterized by certain kinds of delusions, hallucinations, and/or thought disorders. Third, there must be other specific evidence of poor prognosis, such as early onset, or poor premorbid adjustment. In addition, other psychoses such as depression must be ruled out. The Feighner criteria actually diagnose as "true" schizophrenics only those patients previously diagnosed as chronic schizophrenics. This diagnostic approach identifies the most chronically ill and most hopeless patients, the patients called "nuclear" or "process" in the past, the patients least likely to remit and least likely to benefit from treatment. For whatever reason, this particular system, so different from all previous approaches of the twentieth century, has been very enthusiastically received.

The Research Diagnostic Criteria (Spitzer, Endicott, and Robins, 1978) is an elaboration of the Feighner Criteria. It differs basically in two ways. First, the duration of only two weeks rather than six months is required. And second, the symptoms required for the two-week period are more elaborately detailed. The patient must have two of eight symptoms listed. The first seven are either the Schneiderian first-rank symptoms themselves, derivatives of them, or combinations of symptoms similar to those of the Schneiderian system. The eighth is the Bleulerian thought disorder, if accompanied by psychoses, inappropriate affect, or disorganization.

The New Haven Schizophrenic Index and the Flexible System for the diagnosis of schizophrenia have had little or no influence on the current official diagnostic system, *DSM-III*. The Feighner system and the Research Diagnostic Criteria are basically the precursors to *DSM-III*. In fact, *DSM-III* is largely a combination of these two approaches. Fenton, Mosher, and Matthews (1981) upon comparing these four systems with Schneider's conceptualization of first-rank symptoms and *DSM-III*, concluded that, although these systems provided reliability, they did not provide construct validity. Thus, none would identify "true" schizophrenia and none was much more useful than any other.

DSM-I and *DSM-II*

The *DSM-I* definition of schizophrenia (American Psychiatric Association 1952) emphasizes disturbances in reality testing, thought processes, affect, intellectual functioning, and regressive behavior. It provides a broad definition, noting that the disturbances can present themselves in varying degrees and mixtures. Although *DSM-I* seems most definitively influenced by Bleuler, it also shows the mark of the ego psychologists in its consideration of a number of ego functions. In addition, the emphasis on the retreat from reality and on regression possibly shows a psychoanalytic influence.

DSM-II (American Psychiatric Association 1968) describes schizophrenia as manifested in characteristic disturbances in thinking, mood, and behavior. Its description is similar to that of *DSM-I*, continuing to provide a broad definition. The Bleulerian influence has increased, however: the thought disorder is now clearly considered the primary underlying disturbance, and all of Bleuler's four *As* are described. Basically, *DSM-II* can be thought of as a derivative of Bleuler.

DSM-III

The contrast between *DSM-I* and *DSM-II* and the present classification, *DSM-III* (American Psychiatric Association 1980), is striking. *DSM-III* is definitively influenced by its immediate precursors, the Feighner criteria and the Research Diagnostic Criteria. The *DSM-III* diagnosis of schizophrenia includes six different criteria. First, one of six symptoms must be clearly present. As in the Feighner criteria, the first five symptoms are either the Schneiderian first-rank symptoms themselves, derivatives of them, or at least combinations of symptoms that seem strikingly similar to those of the Schneiderian system. The sixth symptom is basically the Bleulerian thought disorder, if accompanied by blunted, flat, or inappropriate affect, psychoses, or disorganized behavior. Second, a deterioration from previous functioning is required. Third, the symptoms must be continuous for at least six months during some time in the patient's life. Part of the six-month period can include a prodromal and/or residual phase. Fourth, if there is depression or mania, it must be clearly secondary to the schizophrenic symptoms. Fifth, onset must be before age 45. And sixth, organicity must be ruled out.

One can think of *DSM-III* as a derivative of the combined theories of Kraepelin, Schneider, and Bleuler. Kraepelin and Schneider are seen as primary, with Bleuler taking a somewhat secondary position. There is no influence from ego psychology or from any psychodynamic conceptualization. *DSM-III* provides a narrow conception of schizophrenia, making it similar to the European models. It presents a precise and easy method of making the diagnosis, providing a system that is easily used for research.

The definition is so narrow that it excludes the vast majority of patients diagnosed as schizophrenic in the past. Like the Feighner criteria, it includes patients similar to those diagnosed as schizophrenic using the Kraepelinian system. This group corresponds to a group previously called "nuclear" or "process," a group with the worst possible prognosis. This extremely narrow definition seems to imply a genetic understanding of schizophrenia, yet there is some indication (Gottesman and Shields 1972) that this kind of narrow system would not tend to identify those patients in whom any existing genetic factor was operating.

DSM-III also shifts from a focus on Bleuler to a focus on Schneider. The advantage of this shift seems unclear. Recent research (Pope and Lipinski 1978, Pope, Lipinski, Cohen, et al. 1980, Procci 1976) indicates, however, that neither Bleuler's thought disorder nor Schneider's first-rank symptoms are by themselves pathognomonic for schizophrenia. Completely eliminating the influence of the ego psychologists (and other psychodynamic theorists) weakens the system. The ego psychological approach, by examining an inventory of different ego functions, can provide a very precise delineation of both strengths and weaknesses in any given patient. Such information has clear utility in therapeutic consideration and intervention. *DSM-III* does not provide this focus; it sees schizophrenia basically as a diagnosis of severe weaknesses only and thus implies therapeutic nihilism. In addition, other writings (Fenton, Mosher, and Matthews 1981, Overall and Hollister 1979) foster the conclusion that *DSM-III* provides arbitrary diagnostic criteria.

DSM-III should be accepted as only one system, among many, for making the diagnosis of schizophrenia. It does not provide construct validity, it identifies only the most chronic schizophrenics it does not provide either genetic or psychodynamic understanding, and it implies therapeutic nihilism. When one evaluates a patient for schizophrenia, *DSM-III* should be consulted but not considered the final word.

Conclusion

The diagnosis of schizophrenia remains as difficult and controversial as ever. In attempting to make the diagnosis, one should examine as many relevant approaches and factors as possible. In addition to *DSM-III*, one might look at other diagnostic systems, certainly including Bleuler's. A detailed evaluation of the patient's ego functioning is invaluable. In addition, such factors as the patient's developmental history, current environmental stresses, genetic background, and relationship to the interviewer might be considered. Only after all these areas are thoroughly examined would one be in a position to make an assessment of the patient's psychopathology or to make the diagnosis of schizophrenia.

PART FOUR

Treatment

CHAPTER 14

Clinical Case Studies

This chapter will present six case studies in which the diagnosis of borderline personality should be considered. The borderline group consists of a great variety of individuals, with widely different personalities and widely different behaviors. What enables one to classify such different individuals as borderline personalities is the characteristic profile of relative ego strengths and underlying ego weaknesses. Even the use of this ego psychological diagnostic approach, however, leaves "gray areas". Several patients described in this chapter are either on the border between borderline and neurotic or between borderline and psychotic conditions. Additionally, one of the six patients is thought to be a narcissistic personality. All cases are scrutinized by the ego psychological diagnostic approach. The interactions and life histories of these patients are used to demonstrate each patient's ego strengths and ego weaknesses. The composite ego profile of each patient is subsequently discussed and used to determine whether the diagnosis of borderline personality is justified. The ego profile helps compare the diagnosis arrived at using the ego psychological diagnostic approach with that derived through other approaches.

CASE 1: MS. W

Ms. W was a 23-year-old single woman, a recent college graduate now working as a librarian at a local university. She initially presented a long list of problems. She expressed most difficulty with her fluctuating moods. Little things affected her easily, and she frequently became annoyed, angered, or depressed, especially in response to perceived slights and rejections. At times she experienced explosive rage. Recently, for example, she had torn up a number of her books and papers in a "violent" episode. At times she felt bored, "numb," or even "dead." She often initiated dangerous activities to ward off these uncomfortable feelings. She had a history of shoplifting and now "enjoyed" reckless speeding in her car. On occasions she had put her hand through windows and pounded her fists on the wall. She sometimes used marijuana and alcohol, as well as eating binges, to lessen these feelings. Sometimes during these "agitated" times, Ms. W felt disorganized and clearly "out of control." There were also less severe "disturbed" periods when she felt somewhat strange and isolated, had difficulty concentrating, and felt as if she were "losing her thoughts." Ms. W came for a consultation because she wanted to exercise "more control over her moods" and thinking processes and wanted to obtain a more integrated life. She was not satisfied with her current job, nor was she pleased with her current social situation. She did not feel like a "whole" person and was not sure who she was, what life was about, or in what direction her life was going.

Ms. W had done very well at an excellent midwestern liberal arts college, where she had majored in English literature. She felt that although her current job as a librarian certainly provided a useful function, it was lacking in stimulation—in fact, it was quite dull. She yearned for the academic stimulation of college but was unable to find employment that provided that kind of "excitement."

Her social life she found totally unsatisfactory. She had been "going with" a 24-year-old graduate student in business administration for a number of months. She and her boyfriend were continually together, having a relationship that seemed quite excellent on the surface. They talked well with each other, seemed to have a good time together, had similar interests, and were very compatible sexually. Intercourse occurred regularly, and Ms. W enjoyed the act and was orgasmic. Despite all this, Ms. W constantly questioned her relationship with her boyfriend. She did not experience any "real" feelings toward him and did not have an understanding of him as a person. She did not even know if she liked him. She viewed him as someone to be with, someone to "soothe" her and to help prevent the occurrence of boredom and other uncomfortable affect states. Recognizing this situation, she felt she was "using" him and often thought she should end the relationship.

Ms. W had met her boyfriend when he visited the library where she worked. He became very rapidly attracted to her, physically, sexually, and intellectually. Although she did not experience any feelings for him, Ms. W acted as if she liked him quite a bit and was very willing to date him frequently and to become sexually involved with him. As noted, something about him "soothed" and "pacified" her; she did not experience the same emotional turmoil with him that she had felt with other boyfriends. Ms. W's usual dating pattern was to become involved with one man at a time, usually for a number of months. She had had a large number of "close" relationships of this nature for a number of years now. Basically all the relationships were similar. Ms. W acted as if she liked the men but could neither experience feelings toward them nor conceptualize them as people. She used the various men to help ward off boredom and other unpleasant affects, but this attempt was often unsuccessful. The typical relationship was considerably more stormy than the one just described.

Ms. W was very sensitive to slights and rejections and constantly responded to them with emotional outbursts. Crying spells, rage attacks, physical fights, self-destructive behavior, binge eating, and excessive alcohol and drug use were commonplace. At times, when Ms. W was feeling particularly "bored," "empty," or "dead," she would initiate quarrels with her boyfriends that would easily and quickly lead to these kinds of emotional outbursts.

Ms. W was exceptionally attractive, intellectual, and sexually interested, and she had no difficulty putting on an "act" of liking the men she dated. As a result, she was very popular despite her excessive emotionality. In fact, she was always the one to end her relationships. Although she often expressed guilt about using her boyfriends, she seemed to terminate her relationships not because of this guilt but, rather, when she felt bored and had found another relationship that looked more exciting and stimulating. From high school on, Ms. W had had one relationship of the kind described after another. She basically had no close women friends over this period of time.

Ms. W had been born and raised in a small city in the northwest. Her father, a prosperous businessman, had been out of town more often than he was present. He favored Ms. W, his most attractive daughter, and was very seductive to her at times. Ms. W alternated in idolizing him and wanting nothing to do with him. Her mother, with whom Ms. W had been very close in her early years, was described as explosive, always yelling and shouting at the children and always threatening divorce. Ms. W basically avoided her at present. There were five daughters and two sons in the family. Ms. W had been very "close" to her siblings as a child but now had little to do with them except when she visited home. She did seem to retain a keen sense of sibling rivalry with several of her sisters, particularly in regard to receiving money and other gifts from her father. Ms. W described her parents and siblings solely in terms of their relationship with her. Pictures of them as independent individuals in their own right did not emerge during the interviews.

Ms. W had used her exceptional intelligence to do relatively well throughout school. In college she had found some of her schoolwork stimulating and actually had been able to use this work as another way of dealing with her upsetting emotional states. This was particularly true of English literature; Ms. W had become excited and "stimulated" by a variety of novels. Mostly because of this involvement with her schoolwork, Ms. W's college life had been less stormy than her high school years, yet stormy enough by any other standard. Ms. W had never developed close individual friendships; she often traveled in groups, "acting" interested in the various group activities. She had become involved quite early in the intense dating pattern already described. Ms. W presented her chief complaints as chronic problems that had been going on for years. She had sought psychotherapy on two previous occasions but each time had left after a month or two, feeling that she had benefitted little and that in fact her life was "not all that bad."

Ms. W was a slender, very attractive young woman, always dressing stylishly and looking a bit younger than her age. She talked in a kind of affected way, with a mild British-like accent. She was always polite, somewhat formal, and somewhat stilted. She showed little affect, although she would frequently break out in heavy laughter when she spoke of her problems. The formality, isolation, and intellectualization during the interviews was in marked contrast to her main complaints of difficulties with fluctuating moods, overwhelming affect states, and acting-out behavior. This "formal" appearance was the way Ms. W most often presented herself when not under stress. This presentation had a quality of falseness to it, a quality of concealing a different underlying personality. Ms. W talked eloquently and correctly and had a tendency to use esoteric vocabulary. She certainly showed no problems in conceptual thinking during the interviews.

An ego psychological diagnostic approach to this case would proceed as follows. Although she experienced disorganization and derealization under acute stress, Ms. W always was able to maintain reality testing. Likewise, although she felt she was "losing her thoughts" and experienced loss of control of her thinking processes under stress, her thinking actually remained on a secondary process level at all times. Thus, reality testing and thought processes in Ms. W were both basically strong. We can next consider Ms. W's interpersonal relations. On the surface she had many "friends" and acquaintances. As she herself would readily admit, however, these people were not experienced as individuals in their own right. Rather, they were seen as objects, filling definite needs in Ms. W's life, easily interchangeable with one another. Ms. W established no long-term relationships and was even distant from her parents and siblings. Surface functioning in adaptation to reality was quite good. Ms. W had done well in college and currently had a decent job. Her social life was chaotic, however, and there was little goal direction in either her work or her social life.

The most glaring problems with Ms. W involved frustration tolerance and impulse control, as well as affective stability. Ms. W was very sensitive to slights and rejections, responding easily to frustration with a variety of disruptive emotional outbursts and impulsive acts. Ms. W's life was filled with such unpleasant affect states as agitation, rage, boredom, emptiness, and "deadness." Primitive defenses were seen both in day-to-day functioning and under stress. Most common among these was acting out. Some evidence of splitting and related defenses could be seen in Ms. W's relationship with her parents. With her acquaintances, Ms. W maintained enough distance so that the more primitive defenses were not apparent. The main defenses here included a kind of isolation, a kind of depersonalization, a "protective" distancing, and a superficial conviviality and compliance together with a kind of internal withdrawal. Ms. W also used intellectualization, reaction formation, flight into activity, and displacement in her daily life. In her ability to channel her energies into creative enjoyment in English literature, she seemed to be using sublimation, a mature defense. Evidence of identity diffusion was clear. Ms. W presented a kind of superficial sense of self, convivial and compliant, and a pretense of being interested in various activities. Yet this facade was stilted and clearly lacking in genuineness. Underneath, Ms. W experienced a lack of a self; she really had no feeling about who she was. Analogously, she experienced no feelings for other people, was unable to describe people she knew in any meaningful way, and related to others almost exclusively as if they were objects. An integrated, cohesive sense of self and objects was clearly lacking in Ms. W.

Thus, an ego psychological diagnostic approach, when applied to Ms. W, shows a pattern of strong reality testing and strong thought process, interpersonal relations that initially look adequate but that are almost exclusively need fulfilling, and adaptation to reality that is adequate but far from optimal.

Frustration tolerance and impulse control are poor. There is a tendency to use some primitive defenses, particularly acting out, in both day-to-day functioning and under stress, in combination with a wide variety of more neurotic defenses. Defenses related to splitting are in evidence but not prominent. One mature defense, sublimation, is used on a fairly regular basis. Identity diffusion is clear, and affective instability is marked.

From an ego psychological point of view, Ms. W most clearly fits into the borderline group. Ms. W's defensive pattern seems less primitive than that of many borderline individuals. She uses a mature defense regularly, something thought by some to be unusual in borderline individuals. The ego psychological diagnostic approach is very helpful here in focusing on this defensive pattern, a pattern that becomes particularly important when prognosis and therapeutic interventions are considered. Ms. W probably presents an example of an individual who can be diagnosed as a borderline personality without much controversy. Yet her narcissistic vulnerability, her proclivity for disruptive pathological feeling states, and her difficulty with maintaining significant relations might lead Kohut to wonder if she would qualify as a narcissistic personality. Noting her affective instability and proclivity for emotional outbursts, Donald Klein might place her into one of his categories of affective illness and prescribe medication. Ms. W seems to fit into several subgroups in Meissner's categorization. Her compliant facade and protective withdrawal are in accordance with the description of the false self, yet her marked affective components are more in accordance with some of the entities on Meissner's hysterical continuum.

CASE 2: MRS. R

Mrs. R was a 42-year-old woman, married for twenty years and currently living with her husband, her 19-year-old son, and her 17-year-old daughter. The first evaluation session took place in the interviewing room on a short-term psychiatry unit at a local hospital. Mrs. R was cordial, warm, and very talkative through-out the interview. She complained that her husband had been distant to her for several months. A week prior her mother-in-law had come for a visit, and Mrs. R felt that her husband had become even more detached from her at that time while becoming increasingly affectionate with his mother. To her own surprise, Mrs. R also felt "emotionally drawn" to her mother-in-law, while beginning to hate her husband. She now felt that her husband was an evil spirit, in direct communication with Satan and the communists. She felt that her husband, in conjunction with Satan and the communists, had implanted electrodes in her head. It was of crucial importance that the government know about this immediately. Mrs. R had attacked her husband earlier that day, when she felt he was influencing her via the electrodes. The ideas about the electrodes, Satan, and the communists had first come to her early that morning, shortly after awakening. These thoughts did not "bother" her now, eight hours later, nearly as much as previously.

A second interview, the next day, found Mrs. R again to be in good spirits, warm, and talkative. She no longer had thoughts about the electrodes, Satan, or the communists. She now did not understand where those ideas had come from. She did feel that she hated her husband, however, and never wanted to see him again. She felt it was inconsiderate of him to have invited his mother to the house without consulting her first. She stated that her husband was cold, mean, and indifferent. She did not understand how she had remained married to him for twenty years, and she wanted an immediate divorce.

Mrs. R had met her husband when she was 21 years old. At that time she was involved in an emotionally "chaotic" re-lationship with her own mother. She felt that she actually went to her husband more to get away from her mother than because of her attraction to him. She had been attracted to him, however, finding him smart, handsome, and especially kind to her. He had said nice things to her, bought her things, and treated her in a way that she had not encountered before. Sex had been pleasurable, although Mrs. R was not orgasmic. Feeling that her husband was the "nicest" man she had ever met, Mrs. R had married him within a year. Mr. R was an economist for the government, two years older than Mrs. R, and had been "searching" unsuccessfully for a wife for a number of years. Mrs. R's "earthy" personality, her warmth, and her attraction to him had pleased him very much.

The marriage had been initially successful, with the early arrival of two children filling a central role in the lives of both Mrs. R and her husband. When the children became older, Mrs. R had found herself with more free time and had obtained a part-time job as a receptionist-secretary, a job that she held for a number of years. At times Mrs. R did not find her husband to be as kind and considerate as she initially perceived him to be. In fact, there were times, often when he was preoccupied with his career, that she found him to be cold and distant. At these times Mrs. R often began to feel that he was having affairs with other women; on occasion she became fleetingly convinced of his infidelity. Mrs. R also experienced difficulties with her mother-in-law's visits. Her husband had always been exceptionally close to his mother, and Mrs. R typically felt left out, rejected, and unloved by her husband during these visits. At these times Mrs. R began to experience her husband as a bad person. She "hated" him and wanted nothing to do with him. It was at these times, when Mrs. R felt rejected, hurt, and neglected, that she had psychotic episodes. These episodes occurred at times when Mrs. R experienced her husband as cold and indifferent, more interested in his job than in her, having affairs with other women, and preferring his mother to her as a source of emotional support.

Mrs. R had had eight transient psychotic episodes over the prior twenty years. All seemed precipitated by feelings of hurt and rejection in relation to her husband. The longest episode had lasted two full days, but most were less than a day in duration. Mrs. R usually sought brief hospitalization and basically recovered spontaneously. Medication was not used during the episode described here. Although major tranquilizers had been administered during a number of the previous episodes, it is doubtful that they were necessary. During all the psychotic periods, Mrs. R viewed her husband as a terrible person and wanted an immediate separation. During all the episodes she was regressed, often assaultive to her husband,

and frankly delusional. Once the psychotic episode had sub-
sided, a typical pattern would emerge. Initially Mrs. R would
continue to view her husband as a bad person, wanting nothing
to do with him. She would remain in the house but would move
to the guest room in the basement. Gradually she would change
her mind about her husband and finally would move back into
the bedroom. Often there was a brief period when she and her
husband slept in different beds. Usually within several months
they were back to their "usual" relationship.

Between psychotic episodes, Mrs. R functioned basically as
a "normal," although highly neurotic, woman. She did an
excellent job raising her children and was able to do good work
for a number of years in the receptionist-secretarial job. She
was a warm and giving woman, liked by many, but had no close
long-term friendships outside her family. She tended to form
romantic, idealized fantasy relationships with men with whom
she worked, but these remained in fantasy. She sometimes
became easily upset, usually in response to perceived slights by
her husband. At these times she would typically become
involved in numerous structured activities to help ward off
anxiety. On occasion her days would be scheduled from dawn
to dusk and she would be seen "running around" in a kind of
frenzied, highly emotional state. At these times she was quite
vulnerable to affective outbursts of rage or depression. Such
"frenzied" periods usually preceded her psychotic episodes, but
often she was able to revert to "normal" without the occurrence
of such an episode. Mrs. R was also vulnerable to mini-
paranoid feelings, usually involving ideas about her husband
having affairs. She also evidenced a number of isolated
phobias, refusing to use elevators or to fly in airplanes. At times
she would become very preoccupied with her health, feeling as
if she were "coming down" with one disease after another.

Mrs. R had been born and raised in New York City. Her
father had died when she was 2 years old. After his death she
had been raised solely by her mother, a woman described by
Mrs. R as very intrusive, highly emotional, rigid, and demanding. There was a brother 2 years older, with whom Mrs. R
had been very close as a child and adolescent. He had moved to
California a number of years prior and no longer maintained

much contact with Mrs. R. Mrs. R had lived for most of her life with her mother and brother, except for two brief periods when she stayed with an aunt, while her mother was hospitalized for what sounded like brief psychotic episodes. Mrs. R had always had a difficult time pleasing her mother. No matter how hard she tried, she always seemed unable to obtain the love and affection she so often desired. During her early years her older brother had been the one who provided much support and affection. Mrs. R had enjoyed school, had been an average student, and had had numerous school "friends." Outside of the school setting, Mrs. R had been allowed out of the house to play with others only occasionally, and thus she had developed no neighborhood friends. Strict limitations also had been placed on Mrs. R's dating behavior, and she had not had her first date until high school graduation. Mrs. R had developed a compliant, pleasant personality early, always trying to please and to gain acceptance and love. She had become increasingly aware of the "difficult" situation with her mother at home but nevertheless had continued to live with her mother for several years after she graduated from high school. Her husband had been the first man with whom she formed any kind of long-term relationship. As noted previously, she had married more to get away from her mother than because of her attraction to him.

Mrs. R was a neatly, although not stylishly, dressed woman of medium height and weight, moderately attractive and looking her stated age. She was always cordial and friendly, and related in a warm manner. She talked easily and at length, with fluency and spontaneity, always remaining goal directed. The qualities of passivity and compliance were very apparent during the initial interviews. During these times, Mrs. R appeared a pleasant woman, very much trying to please. She showed much affect but never became very angry or upset. Even during the first interview, when she was overtly psychotic, she presented herself in this pleasant manner. It seems clear that during the interviews Mrs. R was able to present herself "at her best." The structure and supportive environment of the interview situation, together with Mrs. R's great need to present herself in a way that could elicit love and affection, combined to allow her to act in this manner easily. It also seems clear that Mrs. R, in other day-to-day structured situations, was often able to present herself in a similar way. Only in more stressful situations and long-term relationships would her problem areas become apparent.

An ego psychological diagnostic approach to this patient reveals the following findings. Reality testing, although generally intact in day-to-day functioning, was markedly vulnerable to paranoid distortions and psychotic regressions under stress. Fleeting paranoid distortions, usually readily reversible but sometimes longer lasting, were not uncommon. All the acute psychotic episodes were clearly related to stress, and all were readily reversible within a day or two. Although major tranquilizers were used to abort a number of these episodes, it seems likely that these regressions would have reversed themselves spontaneously without medication. Mrs. R basically used secondary process thinking except during acute psychotic episodes, when primary process thinking came to the surface. Interpersonal relations appeared sound superficially. Mrs. R had numerous acquaintances and a family that had remained intact over many years. She had good relationships with her children, to whom she showed concern, feeling, and affection. Although her relationship with her husband was basically of the need-fulfilling variety, Mrs. R was able to express warmth and concern for him at times. During evaluation sessions, even when overtly psychotic, Mrs. R related in an open, cordial, and warm manner. Adaptation to reality, except during acute psychotic episodes, was quite good.

Evidence of difficulty with frustration tolerance and impulse control, as well as of affective instability, was shown by Mrs. R's vulnerability to various emotional outbursts and by her "frenzied" states under stress. In addition, small amounts of additional frustration led easily to a variety of new symptoms, including phobias, paranoid feelings, hypochondriasis, and increased activity, in addition to the direct discharge of affects. Evaluation of defensive functioning showed a generous use of some of the more primitive defenses alongside many neurotic ones. Of the primitive defenses, primitive idealization, acting out, and projection were particularly prevalent. Splitting was used to some extent and became especially prominent under stress. During the psychotic regressions certain narcissistic defenses were also employed. Some of the more typical neurotic defenses used by Mrs. R included repression, displacement, reaction formation, passivity, and compliance. Identity diffusion was not greatly apparent in Mrs. R. Except during psychotic episodes, Mrs. R basically was able to maintain a stable and integrated image of herself, along with coherent and integrated images of others. Although her self-esteem was fragile and vulnerable to easy regressions, other aspects of her self concept seemed basically integrated and constant. During psychotic regressions Mrs. R's concept of others, notably her husband, would change radically; yet even then she often maintained an integrated concept of herself.

The ego psychological diagnostic approach in this case shows reality testing that is superficially intact yet very vulnerable to distortion and psychotic regression under stress. Thought processes are secondary process in day-to-day functioning but are vulnerable to regression to primary process under acute stress. Interpersonal relations are basically mature, although there is some tendency to form need-fulfilling relationships. Adaptation to reality is certainly good, whereas frustration tolerance and impulse control are episodically poor. There is extensive use of some of the more primitive defenses, both in day-to-day functioning and under stress. Identity diffusion is not marked, whereas affective instability is clearly evident.

Mrs. R easily meets the ego psychological criteria for the diagnosis of borderline personality, except in the areas of interpersonal relations and identity diffusion. Although she does show evidence of some disturbance in these areas, she is basically able to maintain integrated images of herself and others and to attain long-lasting relationships that help provide continuity and meaning to her life. The existence of relatively good interpersonal relations and identity formation in an individual whose overall ego functioning is markedly weak in other areas is not unusual, although it certainly is not typical. This pattern is seen fairly often in both borderline and psychotic individuals. In these individuals there must have been some kind of constancy in early parenting that overrode numerous other early developmental failures. In the case of Mrs. R, it is unclear how she obtained this early constancy.

In the present case, despite the relative strengths in interpersonal relations and identity formation, the overall ego picture certainly warrants a diagnosis of borderline personality by the ego psychological diagnostic approach. Indeed, Mrs. R would probably be judged a borderline individual on the basis of virtually any diagnostic system. Given her vulnerability to distortions and psychotic regressions under stress, some might even entertain a more psychotic diagnosis. This does not seem justified, however. To think of Mrs. R as basically psychotic, one would have to see a more continual expenditure of energy to maintain reality testing. Although Mrs. R is clearly vulnerable to psychotic regressions under stress, under usual circumstances she experiences little difficulty with reality. Mrs. R has a number of features in common with the pseudoschizophrenic group and the psychotic character in Meissner's categorization, although in many ways she appears healthier than the typical patients in these subgroups. In the case of Mrs. R, the diagnosis of borderline personality is fairly easy to establish. The use of the ego psychological diagnostic approach is particularly helpful here in highlighting the ego strengths of interpersonal relations and identity formation. The clear establishment of these strengths in an otherwise basically borderline individual makes understanding, prognosis, and therapeutic planning in this case much different than it would be with many other borderline individuals.

CASE 3: MR. M

Mr. M was a 24-year-old single man, living in a group home and working as a consultant for the government. He came for consultation at the recommendation of his ex-girlfriend, with whom he had lived for two years and from whom he had recently separated. Chief complaints were vague and were presented in a very theoretical and highly abstract fashion. All the complaints were of a chronic nature. They had increased in intensity when Mr. M's mother had died two years prior, however, and again recently after his separation from his girlfriend. Repetitive efforts at focusing were necessary to help Mr. M both establish and elaborate on these chief complaints. Mr. M experienced difficulties in knowing how to "behave" in social situations. He felt that he should act in accordance with what others expected of him, but he was often unsure what was expected. He could not use his own feelings to help him, because he felt very uncertain about what his own feelings were. He especially had difficulty differentiating his own feelings from feelings he felt others expected him to have. As a result, Mr. M experienced his behavior and style of interaction as varying greatly from time to time. He was markedly sensitive and vulnerable to the opinions of others and altered his behavior in accordance with these perceived opinions. He saw himself as having difficulty maintaining goals and direction in life, although he currently had a decent job and was looking forward to applying to law school.

In addition, Mr. M experienced difficulty "sorting out" his thoughts, particularly in deciding what thoughts he should "emphasize." He became confused at times between what he was thinking and what he should be thinking. On occasion he felt "immobilized" and overwhelmed by his "thinking processes." Nevertheless, Mr. M had been an honors student at an excellent college. He always performed well in structured situations, like school, in which the goals were clear, but he felt inadequate in less structured environments, particularly social ones. All of Mr. M's presenting problems were subtle, and, as noted, repeated questioning and focusing were required before they became clear. Mr. M felt upset about the separation from his girlfriend but seemed more "lost" than depressed. Although he acknowledged the chronicity of his problems, he felt that he could attain insight into them, including tracing them back to their childhood origins, in weekly therapy sessions over a period of about nine months. These ideas about psychotherapy he had obtained from his girlfriend.

Mr. M had met his most recent girlfriend several months before the death of his mother. He had fallen rapidly in love with her, although he could not say why or define what he meant by love. Mr. M had been living with his mother for a number of years prior to her death. Upon her death, he had moved in with his girlfriend, a 31-year-old woman, and had lived with her until very recently. He had formed a kind of passive-dependent relationship with this more dominant woman, looking to her for advice and support. He basically modeled his life around her expectations, obtaining a job in accordance with her advice and maintaining few other friendships. Sexual relations were unimportant to Mr. M and occurred infrequently but without problems in performance. Mr. M viewed his girlfriend as very knowledgeable and trustworthy, and as an outstanding woman. He saw her as an ideal woman, much as he had viewed his mother. He maintained this view even after the separation. The relationship with his girlfriend had ended suddenly, when she decided that she wanted to date other men. Mr. M would have preferred to stay with her, possibly marrying her, but he reluctantly had agreed to separate. In accordance with her suggestions, he had moved into a group home and called for a psychiatric consultation. He continued to telephone her a number of times a week. She remained very willing to provide the same kind of support and advice on the phone that she had given when they were living together.

Mr. M had been born and raised in a small midwestern town. He had had a very close relationship with his mother, always looking to her for advice and support and always idealizing her. Mr. M's parents had separated ten years earlier, and he had continued to live with his mother after this time, most recently sharing an apartment with her alone. Mr. M's father, a moderately successful businessman, was described by Mr. M as cold, distant, and aloof. Mr. M felt that his father was not particularly interested in him, and they had not seen each other in a number of years. There were two younger brothers, neither of whom Mr. M was particularly close to. From Mr. M's description, it was very difficult to obtain a clear feeling about his parents or brothers as people. Mr. M described his early years as basically normal and uneventful. He felt they were pleasant and typical, and no particular memories stood out.

Mr. M had always done exceptionally well academically, being an honors student throughout. During his school years he had always had a large number of acquaintances but no really close friends. Typically he would become a member of a larger group of boys, easily adapting himself to the norms of the group. He had always been very active in school activities, including sports. Having been troubled by the issues he initially discussed for as long as he could remember, Mr. M seldom maintained individual friendships, preferring to function as a member of different well-structured groups. Mr. M had not dated until his junior year of college. He never had dated frequently but had managed to have one "intimate" relationship before his most recent girlfriend. Sexual intercourse had occurred only with the recent girlfriend. Masturbation was infrequent and was sometimes accompanied by conscious fantasies of a romantic nature, involving older women.

Mr. M, very thin, was always preoccupied with his weight. He desired to gain weight to achieve a more dominant appearance but had difficulty in doing so. For a while he had gone to macrobiotic classes to attain "better metabolism," gain weight, and become more assertive. After college Mr. M had been unclear about his future. He considered either joining a group that was to build a new temple in California or going to a commune in Arizona. He had also contemplated going to law school but instead had taken a government consulting job. During college Mr. M had become intensely involved in transcendental meditation, spending several hours a day meditating for several years. He had stopped when he came to feel that this activity was in fact making him feel more isolated than before. Recently he had been thinking about entering the Church of Scientology.

Mr. M was a tall, quite thin young man, always neatly and fashionably dressed. He was always friendly and very willing to talk. He smiled frequently, always demonstrated a polite manner, and appeared somewhat passive. Although willing and able to talk, he did not always know what to say. Although he was basically goal directed, he would ramble at times and occasionally become confused as to what his thoughts were. He had the tendency to focus on details and to make numerous theoretical abstractions. He was often vague and certainly not well focused. Mood was neutral, and affect was slightly constricted. An optimistic attitude about almost everything was always present.

If we take an ego psychological diagnostic approach to this case, we can note the following. Mr. M's reality testing was basically intact in both structured and nonstructured situations. Thought processes were intact in day-to-day functioning but showed some confusion under stress, particularly in unstructured social settings. Difficulties in this area warranted notice but seemed to be a function of anxiety. The problems were certainly not severe enough to cause one to hypothesize the existence of a thought disorder. Interpersonal relations were superficially intact in that Mr. M maintained a number of acquaintances. He never had close friends, however, basically maintaining a distance between himself and others. The only long-term relationship on which Mr. M focused, the one with his most recent girlfriend, seemed to be basically of a need-fulfilling variety. Adaptation to reality seemed adequate although lacking in goal direction and clearly far from optimal, given Mr. M's intellectual abilities.

Frustration tolerance and impulse control were quite good. There were not even subtle difficulties in this area. There was at lease some evidence of the use of primitive defenses. Mr. M's most typical defenses included isolation, intellectualization, rationalization, reaction formation, the use of vagueness and abstractions, and passivity, together with some primitive idealization, denial, and externalization. The primitive idealization, which Mr. M was able to maintain for long periods, was particularly apparent in his relationship with his girlfriend and his mother. Denial was evidenced in Mr. M's kind of blind optimism, which influenced his judgment at times. The primitive defenses were clearly present but certainly not overwhelming. Thus, Mr. M's usual defenses were of both neurotic and borderline types. Mr. M demonstrated characteristically the syndrome of identity diffusion. He readily changed his presentation of himself under the influence of others, displaying what has been called a chameleonlike identity. His lifelong pattern was to become very involved with and under the influence of numerous groups, to which he would adhere for varying periods of time in an effort to gain a sense of identity. This trait was shown in its most exaggerated form in his excursions into transcendental meditation and macrobiotics, and in his temptations to become involved in Scientology, the new temple in California, and the commune in Arizona. The one close relationship in his life, that with his ex-girlfriend, served a function analogous to that of the groups. Mr. M's concept of himself was vague and shifting, certainly very lacking in consolidation and cohesiveness. Mr. M was unable to characterize significant others in depth. The people he described came across basically as stereotypes. Mr. M did not show significant problems with affective stability. Under the influence of extensive denial, he maintained a good mood and sense of optimism. Mood swings were uncharacteristic of him, as were any kinds of affective outbursts.

Thus, the ego psychological diagnostic approach here demonstrates a pattern of strong reality testing, strong impulse control and frustration tolerance, and no problem with affective stability. Identity diffusion is characteristic and clear-cut. The usual defensive functioning includes both neurotic and borderline defenses. Thought processes are basically intact, although there is certainly evidence of some vulnerability. Interpersonal relations are superficially intact but appear to be basically of a need-fulfilling variety. Adaptation to reality is adequate but far from optimal, considering Mr. M's intellectual abilities. Mr. M is one of many individuals who clearly meets some of the ego psychological criteria for a diagnosis of borderline personality while failing to meet others. It is a "borderline" decision whether to call Mr. M a borderline patient. The overwhelming evidence of identity diffusion, together with indications of the use of some borderline defenses, some vulnerability in thought processes, an adaptation less than optimal, and the problems noted in interpersonal relations, supports the diagnosis of borderline personality. Yet a diagnosis such as passive-dependent personality with marked obsessive-compulsive, narcissistic, and borderline features is not unfeasible.

Mr. M is probably in the borderline group but is functioning at a level approaching that of a neurotic. Kernberg, focusing on identity diffusion, use of primitive defenses, and the intactness of reality testing, would probably call Mr. M a borderline patient. Meissner could easily place Mr. M into the category of dysphoric personality, clearly on the healthier end of the spectrum. In addition, Mr. M basically meets Meissner's criteria for the "as-if" personality. Abend, Porder, and Willick would probably call Mr. M a borderline personality. Kohut, noting Mr. M's vague and ill-defined chief complaints, his narcissistic vulnerability, his difficulties with interpersonal relations, and his work and sexual inhibitions, might deem Mr. M a narcissistic personality. Kernberg certainly would not.

Mr. M is surely one of those many individuals who creates confusion in reference to the diagnosis of borderline personality. He is, in fact, at the border of borderline and neurotic conditions. By applying the ego psychological diagnostic approach, one can derive a detailed ego profile. This profile reveals clearly an individual more troubled than the typical neurotic and certainly presenting many borderline features. The question is whether there are enough borderline features to warrant the borderline diagnosis. Whether or not Mr. M is called a borderline personality, the ego psychological diagnostic approach provides all the necessary information to debate the diagnosis, to begin to understand the individual, to have a good idea of the prognosis, and to initiate therapeutic intervention.

CASE 4: MR. A

Mr. A was a 44-year-old man, divorced for a number of years, living by himself, and currently employed as a construction worker. He came for consultation at the insistence of his supervisor, who told Mr. A that he would lose his job if he did not seek professional help. Mr. A did not feel that he had any personal problems; rather, he felt that his supervisor did not like him and wanted to have him fired. He came for the consultation reluctantly, basically because of the encouragement of his mother. Mr. A felt that his immediate supervisor was putting excessive pressure on him on the job, that this supervisor singled him out for the most difficult work and constantly gave him a "hard time." Mr. A referred to this treatment as harassment and felt that it was increasing to a level that made going to work almost intolerable. Mr. A felt that a number of his co-workers, initially friendly to him, had become critical and "mean" to him of late. He felt that his supervisor must have had something to do with this. Mr. A had held the same construction job for over two years and believed that he had performed admirably. He felt that the harassment had begun several months prior, immediately after a period during which he had become especially close to his supervisor. Because of the harassment, Mr. A had developed a number of symptoms. He had become very preoccupied and obsessed with the work situation, thinking and brooding about it continually. He fantasized numerous ways of getting revenge on his supervisor, including throwing a beer in his face and threatening him on the phone. In addition, Mr. A had developed mild insomnia and anorexia, felt more depressed than usual, and had increased his already moderate-to-heavy alcohol consumption. Mr. A had told a co-worker about his difficulties. The co-worker, in turn, told the supervisor, who subsequently confronted Mr. A, insisting on his seeking professional help.

Over the prior 15 to 20 years, Mr. A had held a series of different jobs, basically clerical, maintenance, and, most recently, construction. Jobs usually lasted a year or two and often ended when Mr. A experienced difficulty getting along with either his peers or his supervisors. There had been several job situations highly similar to the present one, in which Mr. A felt that he was being picked on, treated unfairly, or harassed. Mr. A on several occasions had developed symptoms similar to the present ones in response to the supposed harassment. He had usually quit the jobs upon becoming afraid that he might act out some of his aggressive fantasies. Mr. A was a quiet, very hard-working employee. He did not relate much to his co-workers yet was basically liked by his peers and employers. His employers were usually surprised when Mr. A quit his jobs. The pattern of feeling harassed after allowing himself to become somewhat close to his supervisors was apparent in Mr. A, although he had never noticed this relationship.

For a number of years Mr. A had been somewhat a loner. He lived by himself in an inexpensive apartment, spending most of his free time watching television, reading newspapers, and drinking beer at bars. When inebriated he became much more comfortable and sociable with other people, engaging more easily in conversation. He developed a number of transient "drinking buddies" but no long-term relationships. He had no women friends, having stopped dating a number of years ago. He masturbated regularly, often with sadistic fantasies of inflicting physical pain on his women partners during the sexual act. At age 22 Mr. A had married a very immature woman, 3 years younger than himself. This marriage, lasting about a year and a half, was the longest relationship Mr. A had ever had with a woman. The marriage had been continually marred by arguments and physical fights. Mr. A now had little to say about his ex-wife, except that she was a "bitch" and that the marriage had been a big mistake. When asked to describe her further, he could only add that she was very attractive and totally interested in herself. After the divorce Mr. A dated occasionally but had never formed another long-term relationship with a woman. On several occasions his fantasies during intercourse had become quite violent, scaring Mr. A. He now preferred to have his fantasies while masturbating and had no intentions of dating again. In essence, Mr. A now shied away from both women and men because of his fear of losing control of his aggression.

Mr. A had been born and raised in a medium-sized city in the South. His father, a government worker, was described as cold, indifferent, and mean. He used to beat both Mr. A and his younger brother frequently with a strap or stick for an assortment of "minor" transgressions. Because of his treatment by his father, Mr. A had run away from home on a number of occasions. Mr. A's father had now been divorced for seven years; Mr. A no longer saw him and clearly did not want to. Mr. A described his mother, in contrast to his father, as warm and affectionate, although somewhat overindulgent and overprotective. Mr. A continued to view his mother in the most positive way, having only the nicest things to say about her. She currently lived in the same city as Mr. A, moving there when she felt that he was having difficulties. Mr. A did not have much to say about his brother, 2 years younger and now a mechanic in the southern town where he was born. Mr. A thought that he and his brother had had a "normal" close relationship when younger, but Mr. A was not currently interested in a relationship with him.

In the lower grades Mr. A had presented a number of disciplinary problems. He had got into numerous fights, often had been punished for "acting up" in class, and had played hookey on a number of occasions. There had been one incident of fire setting in school and several at home. Mr. A currently had absolutely no idea what had caused these early problems. In the lower grades he had always been an average student, had actively participated in sports, and had acquired "the usual number" of friends. In high school he had continued to get average grades, although he routinely had cheated on exams. He had developed the habit of lying both in and out of school, often making himself appear "better" by his lies. He had associated with a certain group of boys and had continued to be very active in sports. At that time he felt like "one of the guys," although he never developed very close friends. On several occasions he had got into rather violent fights when he felt that certain boys were picking on him too much. Near the end of high school Mr. A had begun drinking rather heavily, a habit he had maintained since that time. Also in high school, he had begun dating. There had followed a period of several years during which his total interest in dates was to "score," that is, to have sexual intercourse. He had kept track of his total number of "conquests," exaggerated this total to his friends, and saw little use for women outside of sex. After graduating from high school, Mr. A had spent two years in the navy. He had hurt his knee in a "questionable" accident and been discharged with compensation at that time. He had gone to college for one year, studied little, obtained poor grades, and dropped out. He then had begun the series of jobs already described. He had maintained his usual dating pattern until his marriage but had dated less and less after his divorce. Over time, it seemed, he had become progressively more content with fewer and fewer friends and acquaintances.

Mr. A was a tall, mildly obese, middle-aged man, dressed very informally in a somewhat unusual manner. He typically wore shorts, a white T-shirt, sandals, and sunglasses. When asked about his appearance, he simply stated that he felt very comfortable in that outfit. He was basically affable and co-operative during the interviews but was very vague and obscure. In response to confrontations regarding the obscurities, he often became more obscure. Sometimes he rambled and was difficult to follow. Occasionally he became annoyed about a question, being somewhat suspicious about why it had been asked. He usually responded quite favorably to clarifications in this regard. He seemed very serious minded throughout, never smiling and showing little affect. He had little understanding about any aspects of his life, past or present. He did not "think" about the future and subsequently showed little goal direction or motivation. He did not view himself as having problems and had no desire to change.

An ego psychological diagnostic approach in this case reveals the following findings. Although Mr. A's reality testing was very adequate most of the time, there were a number of discrete instances of paranoid distortions. These distortions usually involved Mr. A's supervisors and would occasionally approach delusional proportions. Sometimes Mr. A had great difficulty reversing these distortions spontaneously. The distortions were infrequent, however, and Mr. A had relatively few problems with reality outside of the distortions. Mr. A basically used secondary process thinking. There were some areas of subtle conceptual confusion evident during the interviews, however. These were apparent when Mr. A became vague, obscure, and difficult to follow, and when he became confused about the interviewer's motivations. Interpersonal relations appeared marginally adequate superficially but showed many problems under scrutiny. Because earlier relationships were marred by frightening aggressive fantasies, Mr. A stayed more and more to himself, avoiding interpersonal involvements. He currently had a number of short-term drinking buddies but no long-term relationships. Friendships with women were now nonexistent and never had been other than of the most obvious need-fulfilling variety. Adaptation to reality was superficially intact: Mr. A always was able to work and had some money and a place to live. Mr. A could not maintain a job over time, however, and basically had no goal direction or permanency in his life.

Poor impulse control and frustration were most evident in Mr. A's excessive alcohol intake and his clear tendency to leave jobs and relationships under stress. Evaluation of defensive functioning showed a proclivity to use a number of primitive defenses, alongside a number of neurotic ones. Schizoid withdrawal was becoming a very characteristic defense. Projection was common, sometimes leading to paranoid distortions. Denial was frequently used, and primitive idealization and devaluation were noticeable. Externalization, reaction formation, isolation, vagueness, obscurity, and anger turned against the self were all common. A stable and cohesive identity was clearly lacking in Mr. A. He presented himself as a shallow, stereotyped character leading a simple, uncomplicated life without motivation or goal direction, depth or feeling. He viewed other people in an analogous way: as stereotyped, simple characters lacking depth and personality. In no way did he convey a stable, integrated sense of himself or others. Mr. A displayed severe difficulty with aggression and aggressive fantasies, withdrawing from people and life largely in response to his fleeting awareness of this difficulty. Because of this withdrawal, he was able to maintain an "affective balance" and basically did not demonstrate affective instability.

The ego psychological diagnostic approach as applied in this instance thus reveals reality testing that is grossly intact but clearly subject to paranoid distortions that are at times somewhat difficult to reverse. Thought processes are basically strong, although there is subtle evidence of some disturbance in this area. Interpersonal relations, marginally adequate on the surface, are progressively becoming nonexistent, with those remaining relationships being superficial and clearly of a need-fulfilling variety. Adaptation to reality, although superficially intact, is actually very inadequate. Frustration tolerance and impulse control are clearly poor in several important areas. A number of primitive defenses are regularly used, alongside many neurotic ones. Problems with identity are evident. Affective instability is not overtly displayed, although there are obvious and severe problems with aggression.

Mr. A demonstrates the characteristics of a schizoid personality with paranoid, obsessive-compulsive, and perhaps some antisocial features. According to the ego psychological diagnostic approach, and probably any other diagnostic system, he clearly meets the criteria for a diagnosis of borderline personality. In Meissner's categorization, Mr. A seems to fit into the subgroup of the schizoid personality. The key question here is whether Mr. A is only a borderline patient, or whether he has sufficient problems with reality testing, thought processes, and adaptation to reality to be considered basically psychotic. His deteriorating schizoid withdrawal and his frequent paranoid stance might cause some to think of him as psychotic. Again, the degree of impairment in reality testing and thought processes is crucial here. To think of Mr. A as basically psychotic, one would need to see either a more constant presence of psychotic symptoms, or the necessity for a constant expenditure of energy to maintain reality testing and thought processes and thus avoid psychotic symptoms. Neither of these patterns seems present in Mr. A, although psychological testing would be very helpful in focusing further in this area. Whether Mr. A is a severe borderline individual or a mild psychotic, the detailed elucidation of his ego functioning is of enormous help in understanding him and in establishing an optimal treatment plan.

CASE 5: DR. C

Dr. C was a 27-year-old woman, married for two years and having just moved into the area after completing medical school. She had been in psychotherapy with an elderly woman social worker for the prior three years. She felt that the therapy had been helpful but thought that she clearly needed more therapeutic work. She was initially somewhat vague about her presenting complaints. She said that she was distraught and depressed about the current geographic move, missing her past therapist very much. She had much difficulty with her emotional states in general. She got upset easily, cried frequently, and become enraged at trivial matters. She was particularly sensitive to rejections and slights. She had numerous arguments and fights with her husband, and the future of the marriage now seemed in doubt. She was afraid that she had married her husband for "neurotic" reasons, that he was too much like her father. She felt she loved her husband at times but at other times actually hated him. She had had a series of short affairs since her marriage, often when she found her husband to be too "cold and distant." She drank heavily on occasion and worried about losing control over her drinking. She wanted therapy so that someone could help her to understand herself "totally", to get to the "genetic roots" of her emotions. Despite a promising professional career, she felt that her life was a "mess."

Dr. C had met her husband, a 28-year-old law student, during the third year of medical school, while looking for someone to "screw." Apparently this man strikingly resembled her father, both in physical appearance and in mannerisms. Dr. C had rapidly established an intense emotional and sexual relationship with him, marrying within two months. Her husband, apparently a bit shy and sexually inhibited until he met Dr. C, was described as becoming episodically cold and aloof after the marriage. At these times Dr. C, as noted, would have brief sexual encounters with other men, often men she met at bars while she was mildly intoxicated. Dr. C had been sexually promiscuous for many years now, beginning when she was a teenager. She "enjoyed sex" greatly, participated in a wide variety of sexual activities, was orgasmic, but relied on masochistic fantasies to achieve orgasm. Fantasies usually involved being raped by a number of very virile and aggressive men. Dr. C's usual relationship with a man did not last longer than several weeks. She usually became very attracted to the man she dated, forming a rapid and intense idealization of him. It was not long before she would find some fault with her "friend," however, view him as lacking in some way, and then rapidly end the relationship. Concomitant with the years of stormy social and sexual relationships, Dr. C had been involved in episodic heavy drinking. She felt filled with emotional turbulence and had several mini–depressive episodes. Dr. C had taken overdoses of sleeping medication on two occasions but had not required hospitalization. Through all these events, Dr. C had been able to do exceptionally well in college and to "get by" at medical school. She thought of herself as leading a double life: one as a hard-working professional, another as a "chaotic adolescent."

Dr. C had been born and raised in a large city in the Southwest. Her mother was described as having a "violent temper," beating her frequently during her childhood. Dr. C visualized her mother as a 40-foot monster standing over her. Dr. C now usually "hated" her mother, although at times she viewed her as comforting and supportive. Dr. C described her father as someone with whom she always got into "vehement" arguments. Most recently, on a visit home, she had found herself yelling and cursing him when he "slighted" her intelligence. This behavior was typical of her home visits, and as a result these visits had become infrequent. Dr. C stated that early in life she had idolized her father. Then, when she was 4 years old, her brother had been born, and her father had turned his affection from her to him. She felt that she had been unable to get along with her father ever since. Her younger brother was someone for whom Dr. C had only scorn. She wanted nothing to do with him, nor did she want to say anything about him. It was very difficult for Dr. C to describe her parents or brother except in accordance with her feelings toward them. As a result, it was difficult to obtain a clear picture of them outside of their relationship with her.

Dr. C described her first 4 years of life as idyllic. She viewed her life after this time as having taken a progressively downhill course, becoming more and more filled with emotional turmoil and turbulence. Nevertheless, Dr. C had always performed exceptionally well in school. Greatly aided by her very high intelligence, plus her identification with her father, who was a successful mathematics professor at a small college, Dr. C had been able to split off her academic world from the fury and emotional turmoil that pervaded the rest of her life. She typically had formed idealized relationships with her teachers, and she had used these relationships to help "sustain" her. Occasionally these idealized relationships had changed into very negative ones. Although this pattern had caused occasional reversals in her usually excellent schoolwork, Dr. C had been able to overcome these disruptions without severe consequences. Throughout her life Dr. C had had numerous women "friends." She formed intense "friendships" rapidly but had a habit of ending them just as rapidly, with much emotional upheaval. Nevertheless, Dr. C had been able to maintain several "friendships" for a number of years.

During her second year at medical school, life had become particularly difficult for Dr. C. At this time she had made one of her "suicide gestures" after feeling "humiliated" in pathology class. It was at this time that she had begun psychotherapy with the elderly woman social worker. The psychotherapy had seemed to help stabilize her to some extent, helping her to complete medical school.

The evaluation process with Dr. C became stormy and difficult rapidly. At the initial interview Dr. C wore a stylish dress with stockings and high heels, was neatly groomed, and presented herself in a very intellectual manner. At the second session she wore extremely short, cut-off dungarees and a sleeveless top, and was barefooted. She was very seductive during this session and was filled with emotion, crying and becoming angry at me. When confronted about the difference in her appearance at the two sessions, she explained that she felt very much like two different people. During the first session, she was her professional self; during the second, her "messed-up and chaotic" self. She elaborated that she really did not have a good feeling about who she was, that she felt at times almost like two different people. When I asked Dr. C to elaborate on some of the sexual history she had spontaneously offered, she rapidly became very annoyed with me. She felt that I must be one of those Freudians who were interested only in sex. She further was suspicious that I might be having sexual fantasies about her. She felt that perhaps she should seek out a woman therapist. From this point on, I was perceived in a progressively negative way.

The third appointment took place after Dr. C had returned from a trip to her parents' home. She was enraged at me, stating that the trip had been a catastrophe and that I should have stopped her from going. She had been "humiliated" by her father, with whom she had again engaged in a screaming match. She was feeling particularly distressed because she had called her past therapist and the therapist had not returned her calls. She was also angry at me because I "wasn't that woman therapist." With the help of a number of interpretive and supportive comments, Dr. C was able to calm down and was actually in good spirits by the end of the session. She did not come to the fourth session, and when I called her, she politely told me that she did not think she wanted psychotherapy with a man. She, in fact, had already arranged an appointment with an elderly social worker in the area.

If we take an ego psychological approach here, we can note the following about Dr. C. There were no psychotic episodes or any evidence of problems in self-object differentiation. Distortions of present-day reality based on the infantile past were in great abundance, however. Although some problems involving this subtle defect in reality testing are considered ubiquitous, Dr. C seemed to go beyond the "usual" here. Dr. C basically displayed no problems with thought processes. Regarding interpersonal relations, we can note that Dr. C on the surface interacted with numerous "friends" and acquaintances. There was little evidence, however, that Dr. C viewed these supposed friends as separate individuals having their own separate needs. She described her "friends" in stereotypic fashion and displayed little concern, feeling, or empathy for these people. Her "friends" were basically viewed as objects used by Dr. C in accordance with her needs. The relationship with her husband would certainly fit into this category. Adaptation to reality showed the split that Dr. C noted. On one hand, she was a highly functioning professional; on the other hand, she was a "mess."

The problems that stood out most strikingly with Dr. C were poor frustration tolerance and impulse control, and affective instability. Dr. C's life was characterized by constant emotional storms, with continual angry outbursts, crying spells, and mini-depressions. These emotional storms were always very transient, often occurring in response to perceived slights, rejections, and rebuffs. There was continual acting out, including sexual promiscuity, suicide "gestures," transient relationships, alcohol abuse, and constant activity. Evaluation of defensive functioning showed a definite proclivity to use a number of the more primitive defenses: acting out, externalization, projection, splitting, primitive idealization, and devaluation. These primitive defenses not only were seen throughout Dr. C's day-to-day life but also were very apparent in the evaluation sessions. Nevertheless, Dr. C was able to use typical obsessive-compulsive defenses throughout much of her professional work. Identity diffusion also was clearly displayed in the evaluation interviews as well as throughout Dr. C's life. Dr. C was unable to integrate her sense of self based on her professional career with her more "chaotic" self. She clearly lacked an integrated and cohesive identity, actually viewing herself in numerous contradictory and changing ways. One result was her inability to describe the significant others in her life in other than stereotypic ways.

The ego psychological diagnostic approach as applied in this case reveals reality testing that is grossly intact but subtly defective, strong thought processes, and interpersonal relations that appear adequate on the surface but are basically need fulfilling. A split in the adaptation to reality is evidenced in the concomitant existence of Dr. C's high level of professional functioning and chaotic social functioning. Frustration tolerance and impulse control are frequently poor. There is a definitive proclivity to use a number of the more primitive defenses, together with a variety of more neurotic defenses. Identity diffusion is clearly displayed, and affective instability is marked.

Through use of the ego psychological diagnostic approach, it becomes apparent that Dr. C fits into the borderline group. She represents what has earlier been called an "exceptional" borderline, in that she is able to maximize certain strengths and to adapt well in the structured setting of her professional life, while at the same time displaying chaos in the rest of her life. Dr. C, as would be predicted by the theories of Abend, Porder, and Willick as well as Kernberg, began to develop an intense and chaotic transference even in the evaluation sessions. Also in accord with the theories of Abend and co-workers, Dr. C seemed to display oedipal material. Dr. C would probably fit into the borderline personality proper group of Meissner's classification, although she has a number of characteristics in common with the primitive hysteric. With her vague and ill-defined chief complaints, her narcissistic vulnerability, her proclivity for some pathological feeling states, her perverse sexual fantasies, and her difficulty in favoring long-term, stable relationships, Dr. C might be viewed by Kohut as a narcissistic personality and offered a trial psychoanalysis. Abend and colleagues might also offer such an approach. Donald Klein, in contrast, would probably see Dr. C as fitting into one of his subgroups of affective disorders and would prescribe medication. Again, the detailed focus of the ego psychological diagnostic approach allows one to understand and integrate easily these different approaches to the patient.

CASE 6: MR. D

Mr. D was a 30-year-old man, married for about a year but separated for several months at the time of the interview, who came for evaluation at the suggestion of his wife. His presenting problems were initially very vague and obscure. They seemed to relate to discontent with his separation and the feeling that he was not living up to his potential in life. With directive questioning, it became clear that Mr. D was very unhappy with the separation and very much desired to return to his wife. The separation had been totally his wife's idea, and he felt "forced" to accept it and to adjust as well as he could. Basically, Mrs. D had been bothered by Mr. D's seeming lack of direction in life. She was particularly disturbed by his resistance to change and his "obliviousness" to her concerns about it. Mr. D was usually pleasant, enthusiastic, and vivacious, displayed exceptionally high intelligence, had accumulated several master's degrees, and yet appeared to be going nowhere professionally. In addition, Mr. D occasionally displayed brief periods of uncomfortable brooding and now and then would become enraged, especially when his employer or co-worker seemed to slight his work. These problems were considered minor by his wife, because Mr. D was invariably pleasant when he was with her. Mrs. D "loved" Mr. D but was afraid that he would become a "drifter." This was the story that Mr. D conveyed of the reasons for his wife's suggestion that he seek treatment.

Mr. D himself did not feel at all discontent with life. He minimized his work problems and was very optimistic about his new job, which involved learning about computers. He did not show much concern about his brooding and rage reactions, although he recognized their presence. He felt he was doing well enough in life, although certainly not on the level of his father, the highly successful president of a large bank. Mr. D basically disagreed with his wife's complaints. He very much wanted to remain married to her, however, and wanted to do what was necessary to achieve that end. He was not depressed about his recent separation, although he initially felt very hurt that his wife "would do that to him." He did not actively miss his wife but felt a kind of a void without her. He was less calm and content and missed her "soothing and comforting" presence.

Mr. D had met his wife three years prior, while completing his second master's degree program. Mrs. D, an undergraduate student at the same university, had rapidly become attracted to Mr. D's enthusiasm, pleasantness, vibrancy, and "niceness." Mr. D had been attracted to his wife's looks, her "charm," her stability, and her philosophical commitment to the underdog. They had dated for several years, and then married. Sex was not a "problem," because neither of them greatly desired it. Mr. D stated that he was not greatly sexually inclined, although he did have episodic masochistic fantasies of being forced to have sex by an older and stronger woman. Sex with his wife was infrequent and without any problems in performance. Except for Mrs. D's complaints about Mr. D, the marriage seemed like a pleasant and compatible one.

Academically, Mr. D had always done exceptionally well. He

had been graduated with a major in philosophy and high honors from an outstanding university. He had obtained two different master's degrees in liberal arts areas. A current problem was that he did not know how to convert his academic proficiency into a goal-directed career. The more philosophical and theoretical the subject, the more interested in it Mr. D was. He was not greatly concerned about more "mundane" matters, such as obtaining employment with adequate pay. Mr. D entertained the fantasy that he did not really need to work, that everything would work out well for him anyway. He prided himself on his superior intelligence and academic ability and fantasized that this superiority alone would enable him to do well in life. He secretly looked down on the more ordinary people in the world and considered himself somewhat special and extraordinary. He viewed the mundane life of practical work as "beneath him." All of these thoughts and fantasies Mr. D kept to himself.

Despite his underlying feelings, Mr. D knew that he had to earn a living, and so he, like everyone else, sought employment. With his degrees in intellectual and esoteric areas, he could not find any work appropriate to his academic background. Instead, he was "forced" to obtain a number of jobs: in editing, in government administration, in scientific research, and most recently in computer training. He was never able to keep these jobs for long, however. A repetitive pattern emerged in which, although he "knew" that his work was of superior quality, he felt that either his co-workers or his employer did not offer him the proper respect and, in fact, sometimes belittled or slighted his work. In response Mr. D experienced mildly agitated states, with brooding, physical complaints, and much discomfort. At these times he looked to his wife to soothe and comfort him. On several occasions Mr. D had flown into rages about various situations at work, not in front of his co-workers but in the privacy of his home. He entertained numerous fantasies of plotting to hurt physically those who "insulted" him, but he never seriously considered carrying out any of these plans. Instead, he would calmly go to work and, in a very superior manner, inform his boss that he would no longer be working there. Then he would find himself unemployed for a period of time. Like the feelings and fantasies about himself, Mr. D was usually able to conceal his agitated states from others. He most often was successful in portraying himself in his usual extremely pleasant, optimistic, enthusiastic, and vibrant way. In fact, that was the way Mr. D most often felt about himself.

Mr. D had been born and raised in a large city in North Carolina. His father, now the president of a large bank, highly successful financially and highly influential, clearly had been idolized by Mr. D when he was a child. Mr. D fondly remembered Saturdays, when his father would usually take him around with him on work-related errands, sometimes showing him his places of work, demonstrating to Mr. D how important and influential he was. Although his father spent much less time with Mr. D as the boy grew older, Mr. D had continued to view him as omnipotent and omniscient. Mr. D liked to quote his father, that Mr. D "could do whatever he wanted to do, be whatever he wanted to be." There were "no limits!" His mother, although playing the major role in raising Mr. D, was seen as much less important. A basically pleasant individual, she was an "intellectual," an avid reader, a patron of the arts, and an amateur musician. Both mother and father had constantly emphasized intelligence, academic achievement, and prestige. Mr. D had one brother, 2 years younger than he. When children, they had been very "close," often playing together in preference to having other friends. Mr. D had remained friends with his brother, who at the time was enrolled in a doctoral program in political science in another part of the country.

Mr. D had attended public school in North Carolina and had always done well academically. He had had a number of school "friends" but had tended to play with his brother rather than neighborhood friends. At an early age he had begun to look down on those who did not do very well in school. He had favored boys of his own intellectual ability and preferred his very intellectual brother to the more athletically inclined neighborhood boys. He himself had not participated in sports, preferring to read, write stories, and play games with his brother. Mr. D had been sent away to a boarding school for high school and then had enrolled in the same prestigious college that his father had attended. He had always "loved" school, focusing his main energies into academic and intellectual pursuits. He had become interested in philosophy, religion, and sociology rather early, and loved discussing difficult topics in these areas. With his great emphasis on academics, Mr. D had done little socializing, spending most of his weekends on more "scholarly" matters. At college he had become part of a group of four young men, all with similar "scholarly" interests, spending much time debating various academic issues with them.

Mr. D had not dated until college. At college he had begun to meet and date women sporadically but had formed no close, long-term relationships before meeting his wife. As noted, Mr. D claimed to be minimally interested in sex, although he had masturbated episodically since adolescence, recently with the conscious masochistic fantasies described. After graduating from college, Mr. D had continued his scholarly inclinations by completing two difficult master's degree programs. If it had been practical, Mr. D would have liked to remain in school indefinitely, but after earning the two graduate degrees, he had begun to realize that he needed to earn a living. This need to work was a recent "insight" to Mr. D. During his school years he had been virtually oblivious to it. Mr. D recognized that his schooling had not adequately prepared him for a career but basically did not care. While working at various jobs he always was enrolled in an interesting liberal arts course at the local university.

Mr. D was a good-looking, well-dressed man, somewhat thin, of medium height, wearing horn-rimmed glasses and sporting a mustache. He was quite friendly, very well mannered, and very pleasant. He talked easily and fluently, spontaneously, and in depth. He was basically goal directed, although he became quite vague and abstract at times. He tended to dwell on certain topics, pondering all kinds of details. There was an isolated quality and a mild air of superiority throughout, although Mr. D did show an appropriate amount of affect. Mr. D presented himself as a very mild-mannered and somewhat passive man. He seemed interested in therapy more as an intellectual endeavor than as a means to help himself. He actually seemed content with himself and did not really have a desire to change, except for the goal of returning to his wife.

An ego psychological diagnostic approach applied to this case reveals the following findings. Mr. D showed no problems in reality testing. Thought processes were basically strong, although there was a tendency for vagueness and obscurity at times. Interpersonal relations, clearly good on the surface, were somewhat difficult to evaluate thoroughly. Mr. D always maintained a number of close "friends," some for long periods of time, with whom he shared companionship and intellectual stimulation. One important function of these friends, clearly not consciously recognized by Mr. D, was to help promote feelings about himself as a worthwhile and superior individual. Analogously, an important function of his relationship with his wife was to provide soothing and comforting support when he felt agitated. How far these relationships went beyond the need-fulfilling function was difficult to evaluate in the limited number of sessions. Although adaptation to reality seemed very adequate on the surface, under examination it was far from optimal. Mr. D's tendency to ignore practicality and to pursue only those academic fields that he felt were intellectually stimulating had now made it difficult for him to obtain interesting work. His underlying feelings about his intellectual superiority and his sensitivity to "slights" in this area greatly hampered his work performance and made it difficult for him to hold a job. These same difficulties were now threatening Mr. D's marriage.

As noted, Mr. D was very sensitive to slights and rebuffs in the area of his intellectual ability. His concept of himself as intellectually superior was quite important to him yet seemed to be fragile. Basically unchallenged in this area throughout his life, in academic circles and among his group of friends, Mr. D was now unable to cope with insults to this aspect of himself in the work situation. In this one selected area, Mr. D showed poor frustration tolerance and poor impulse control, along with affective instability. Moderate frustrations here led to agitated states, brooding, physical complaints, and rage reactions. Outside of this selected area, frustration tolerance and impulse control were not areas of difficulty, nor was there evidence of affective instability. Defensive functioning showed a surface pattern of predominantly neurotic defenses. On a more subtle and "concealed" level, however, the concomitant, regular use of some of the more primitive defenses was clearly evident. The primitive defenses most apparent were denial, omnipotence, and devaluation, along with some primitive idealization. The most apparent neurotic defenses included isolation, intellectualization, rationalization, reaction formation, and passivity. There was also a tendency for Mr. D to use one of the mature defenses, sublimation. Mr. D's identity seemed based in part on an underlying concept of himself as an intellectual giant of unlimited ability. He thought of himself as superior to others in this way, and he secretly devalued people who did not live up to his intellectual standards. Covertly, he viewed himself as special, extraordinary, and somewhat "entitled." He felt that his specialness by itself would enable him to lead a comfortable life without much effort. As noted, Mr. D basically kept this concept of himself concealed. Thus, Mr. D's identity, although stable and cohesive, seemed to include an important component based on an underlying grandiose self. The importance of this underlying grandiosity to Mr. D's concept of himself was difficult to evaluate thoroughly during these sessions.

The ego psychological diagnostic approach here reveals strong reality testing and basically strong thought processes. Interpersonal relations, clearly adequate on the surface, are difficult to evaluate in depth. Although they are clearly need fulfilling in many ways, whether they also include higher-level qualities is unclear. Adaptation to reality, clearly adequate superficially, appears far from optimal under scrutiny. Mr. D is very vulnerable to slights and rejections in the area of his concept of himself. In this selected area he displays poor frustration tolerance, poor impulse control, and affective instability. In all other areas these ego functions are basically intact. Mr. D clearly views himself in a grandiose way—as superior, special, and extraordinary—although he generally conceals this concept of himself from others. Thus his identity, although stable and cohesive, seems to include an important component based on an underlying grandiose self. Mr. D employs a basically neurotic pattern of defensive functioning on the surface but in a more concealed way also makes use of some of the more primitive defenses, including denial, omnipotence, devaluation, and primitive idealization.

Via the ego psychological diagnostic approach, Mr. D can be seen to display some borderline features, but he does not fit clearly in the borderline group. Revealing chief complaints that are vague and ill defined, the syndrome of narcissistic vulnerability, some uncomfortable pathological feeling states, a concept of himself based on an underlying grandiosity, at least some problems with work and long-term relationships, a lack of sexual interest, some hypochondriasis, and an underlying sense of entitlement, Mr. D meets Kohut's criteria for a narcissistic personality. It is less clear whether he also meets Kernberg's more stringent criteria. The ego psychological diagnostic approach is most helpful here in showing that Mr. D does not fit clearly into the borderline group, although he does display a number of features more pathological than those of the typical neurotic. The important question is whether Mr. D is basically an obsessive-compulsive neurotic with narcissistic features or a narcissistic personality. A trial psychoanalysis, as recommended by Kohut, would probably be necessary to answer this question definitively.

CHAPTER 15

An Overview of Psychotherapeutic Approaches

Before we examine psychotherapy as used with the borderline patient, we will present an overview of psychotherapy in general. The different types of psychotherapy can be conceptualized on a continuum, with the most insight-oriented and exploratory types at one end and the most supportive types at the other. We will examine four types of psychotherapy along this continuum: psychoanalysis, analytically oriented psychotherapy, dynamically oriented psychotherapy, and supportive psychotherapy. Psychotherapy with the borderline patient will then be related to this continuum. There is a very rich and vast literature (Stone 1951, 1954, Gill 1954, Bibring 1954, Wallerstein 1965, Tarachow 1963, Dewald 1971, Ticho 1970, Kernberg 1980a) differentiating some of these different types of psychotherapies, particularly psychoanalysis and the analytically oriented psychotherapies. This chapter will not attempt to explore this literature in any detail but, rather, will describe and differentiate the various kinds of psychotherapy in an abbreviated way. Parts of this chapter are related to a previous paper (Goldstein 1985c).

Psychoanalysis

The trappings of psychoanalysis involve the patient's coming for regularly scheduled sessions, four or five times a week, for a number of years. There is no contact between patient and psychoanalyst outside of the appointments. Sessions are conducted with the patient lying on the psychoanalytic couch and the analyst sitting comfortably behind the patient. The patient is instructed simply to free associate; that is, he is to do his best to say whatever comes to his mind and not eliminate any thoughts for any reason. He is particularly cautioned to try not to eliminate thoughts because he thinks they are silly or irrelevant, because he is fearful that the analyst will disapprove, because he wants to avoid uncomfortable feelings associated with them, or because the thoughts relate to the analyst. Often this is all the instruction the patient is given.

As the patient tries to free associate, various resistances within him make the process difficult. As these resistances are noticed by the analyst, she will comment on them in an effort to help the patient overcome them and continue to free associate. The analyst initially confines her comments to these resistances and to helping the patient to elaborate and expand on what he is saying. Throughout the psychoanalysis, the analyst's comments remain of a very specific nature. They are directed specifically to the analytic process and are almost always in the nature of clarifications and interpretations. Almost all comments serve the singular purpose of enhancing the psychoanalytic process. Psychoanalysis works as a very gradual process during which aspects of oneself that were previously unconscious become conscious. The transference is used as the primary and most effective forum for this process. In order to provide a setting in which the patient can most easily transfer his feelings onto the analyst, the analyst has to be seen in a neutral way. It is for this reason that the analyst confines her remarks to clarifications and interpretations regarding the psychoanalytic process as exclusively as possible. The analyst is thus able to maintain her "neutral" position while still being warm, empathic, and concerned about the patient.

Aided by the frequency and the intensity of the sessions, by the use of the couch and the basic process of free association, and by the maintenance of a neutral position by the analyst, a progressively intense transference becomes established. This intense transference involves the patient, in a regressed state, displaying or "transferring" onto the analyst feelings and thoughts that were originally directed toward the important people of his early childhood. The transference includes not only these feelings and thoughts, but also defenses against them. It is based on both the actual and fantasized past, as experienced by the patient. The patient's pathological and nonpathological personality traits, as well as his symptoms, all based on intrapsychic conflict, are activated in the psychoanalytic process and become an integral part of the transference. It is the establishment and working through of the transference that is crucial to the attainment of insight, and that most clearly differentiates psychoanalysis from other forms of psychotherapy.

Continuing to confine herself basically to clarifications and interpretations, the analyst begins to comment on aspects of the transference about which the patient is unaware, especially when these appear as resistances to the analytic process. She correlates what is happening in the transference with the patient's current interactions and relationships with significant others, and especially with the patient's significant interactions and relationships in childhood. In this way the analyst helps the patient to begin to learn about previously unconscious aspects of himself, including those aspects that have afforded him the most difficulty. As the patient expands his awareness in this way and gains insight, he is gradually able to make adaptive adjustments and changes in his psychopathology, in his personality, and in his life. The permanency of these changes can be attributed to underlying "structural change," that is, changes in the alignment and relationship of the id, ego, and superego. The analytic process is not smooth; rather, it is characterized by continual resistances and continual progressions and regressions, but with a gradual overall advancement.

Gill (1954), in his classic paper, defined psychoanalysis as a therapeutic technique, employed by a neutral analyst, that permits and results in the development of an intense regressive transference, with the ultimate resolution of this transference by the technique of interpretation alone. There are basically three aspects of this definition that distinguish analysis from other forms of psychotherapy: the analyst's neutrality, the development and resolution of the transference, and the emphasis on interpretation as the primary therapeutic intervention. It is these three aspects that many (Ticho 1970, Kernberg 1980a) focus on when differentiating psychoanalysis from other forms of psychotherapy. Given this definition, for analysis to be successful the patient's personality traits, symptoms, and psychopathology must become activated in the treatment situation, enter into a specific transference with the analyst, and be worked through and resolved in the analytic process by interpretation alone. Thus a critical criterion for analyzability is that such a transference can be formed and resolved without disruptive fragmentation or regression. The basically neurotic individual meets this criterion; the basically psychotic individual does not. Kohut (1966, 1968, 1971, 1977) believes strongly that the narcissistic personality meets this criterion, although many disagree. Whether the borderline individual meets this criterion depends largely on one's criteria for the diagnosis of the borderline personality.

This description of psychoanalysis is meant to be brief. Many of the more technical questions are not addressed here, including such issues as the definition of transference and of the processes of clarification and interpretation, what constitutes neutrality, what exactly is meant by structural change, the definition of insight, and what distinguishes changes via insight from changes via identification.

Psychoanalysis is basically designed for individuals with psychopathology at the neurotic structural level. These individuals include those with symptomatic neuroses but more frequently are people primarily with character (or personality) pathology. They usually suffer from chronic problems that, although far from disabling, interfere with their attaining their life goals, maximizing their potentials, and leading basically content lives. These individuals suffer from a wide assortment of character problems, including those of obsessive-compulsive, hysterical, depressive, masochistic, narcissistic, and mixed natures.

Although the character pathology varies markedly, these individuals commonly present themselves in one of several ways. One of the most common initial presentations is that of the individual who, although he does well on the job and has many friends, is unable to form sustaining, long-term, intimate personal relationships. Marriage is a goal, but something is stopping him from attaining this goal. This individual realizes that his problems are chronic and deep seated and lie within himself. Often he is somewhat sophisticated about psychoanalysis and specifically comes with that treatment modality in mind. This individual frequently, although not always, suffers from sexual difficulties, plus varying degrees of anxiety and depression, in addition to his presenting complaints. A second common initial presentation is that of the patient who, although she performs acceptably at work, feels that something is holding her back and stopping her from living up to her potential. There may be overt problems with her peers or boss, and there may be anxiety about succeeding. This person also has come to realize that her problems are chronic, deep seated, and within herself. She may or may not additionally have problems in maintaining long-term, intimate relationships, and may or may not suffer accompanying anxiety or depression.

For individuals who have psychopathology at the neurotic structural level and who suffer from deep-seated character problems, most obviously manifested in failures in maintaining long-term intimate relationships or in failures in maximizing their potential at work, psychoanalysis is the treatment of choice. This is also the case for individuals with chronic symptomatic neuroses. For individuals who present clear-cut narcissistic problems, psychoanalysis, although recommended by some, remains controversial. Among individuals in the borderline group, psychoanalysis is generally considered only for a selected minority. Psychoanalysis is generally not considered for individuals at the psychotic structural level.

Analytically Oriented Psychotherapy

This chapter will use the terms *analytically oriented psychotherapy* and *dynamically oriented psychotherapy* to describe two different, yet somewhat related, types of therapy. The trappings of analytically oriented psychotherapy involve regularly scheduled sessions, usually two but sometimes three a week, held for varying periods of time. As in psychoanalysis, there is basically no contact between patient and psychotherapist outside of the appointments. Sessions are typically conducted with the patient and therapist sitting across from each other in comfortable chairs. The patient is usually told that the sessions are hers, that she can talk about whatever she chooses. In addition to discussing topics of her choice, the patient is encouraged to report seemingly extraneous thoughts and fantasies that occur to her during the sessions. As in psychoanalysis, areas of typical resistance to such discussion are often mentioned. Thus the trappings of analytically oriented psychotherapy are both similar to and different from those of psychoanalysis.

Although the trappings are somewhat different, the therapist attempts to conduct analytically oriented psychotherapy in a manner as similar as possible to that used in psychoanalysis. He tries to remain neutral, relies on clarifications and interpretations as much as possible, and tries to make maximum therapeutic use of the transference. Just as in psychoanalysis, he comments on resistances, tries to correlate the transference with current interactions and significant childhood relationships, and attempts to help the patient to understand gradually those aspects of herself about which she is unaware. This is analytically oriented psychotherapy in its pure form.

Even this pure form of analytically oriented psychotherapy is usually limited in effectiveness compared with psychoanalysis. With the patient constantly looking at the therapist, noting his expressions and mannerisms, she "learns" more about him than she would in psychoanalysis. She does not see him in as neutral a way and often has more difficulty "transferring" her feelings onto him. Without the use of the couch, without the process of free association, and with less frequent sessions, regression does not occur as easily, and the transference does not usually form with the same primitivity, intensity, or speed. The ability to form a regressed transference varies markedly from patient to patient. Even at its "best," however, the quality of the transference in analytically oriented psychotherapy is rarely on a par with that in psychoanalysis. Although analytically oriented psychotherapy can be quite effective, it is the lack of a fully developed intense and regressed transference that limits this form of psychotherapy.

Recognizing this limitation, some advocate the use of analytically oriented psychotherapy when there is the desire to investigate only selected areas of psychopathology. Certain problem areas are consciously brought into treatment, whereas other areas are consciously omitted. Correspondingly, the focus can include only selected aspects of the transference, with a conscious disregard of other aspects. This modification of the pure form of analytically oriented psychotherapy involves altering the initial instructions to the patient and depends less on the natural development and resolution of the transference. There are many possible modifications of the pure form of analytically oriented psychotherapy. By altering various details regarding the therapeutic focus, the therapist's neutrality, the development and resolution of the transference, and the technical interventions used by the therapist, one can produce countless variations of this form of psychotherapy.

There are basically two groups of individuals who undergo analytically oriented psychotherapy. The first group includes individuals very similar to those undergoing psychoanalysis. Time and money limitations, fears of psychoanalysis per se, and lack of knowledge about the psychoanalytic process are the usual reasons that psychoanalysis proper is not chosen. Almost always this group of individuals would be better off in psychoanalysis. The second group includes individuals for whom analytically oriented psychotherapy, often in a modified form, is the treatment of choice. Included in this group are patients whose potential for regression in psychoanalysis is too great, patients in crises demanding selective therapeutic focuses, patients who will be remaining in the geographic area for only limited periods of time, and patients fearful of or unsophisticated about psychoanalysis who need analytically oriented psychotherapy as preparation for eventual psychoanalysis.

Dynamically Oriented Psychotherapy

The trappings of dynamically oriented psychotherapy involve regularly scheduled sessions, often one but sometimes two a week, held for varying periods of time. There is little contact between patient and psychotherapist outside of the appointments. Sessions are always conducted with the patient and therapist sitting across from each other. Basically the same instructions are given to the patient as in analytically oriented psychotherapy, although sometimes the instruction to report seemingly extraneous material is omitted.

The main difference between dynamically oriented psychotherapy and analytically oriented psychotherapy is the downplaying of the transference as a therapeutic modality in the former. Although transference reactions are noted, especially when they occur as resistances, the elaboration of the transference is not considered a major ingredient in this form of psychotherapy. Rather, the therapist and the patient focus much more exclusively on present-day interactions and relationships, and their correlation to the patient's past. Patient and therapist together try to understand the patient's present-day interactions on the basis of her sensitivities, vulnerabilities, and distortions, which originate in the past. A positive working alliance is fostered, and the therapist is sometimes mildly idealized. Occasional suggestion and education are employed, along with clarifications and partial interpretations, although the former techniques are by no means emphasized. Neutrality is maintained as much as possible.

Dynamically oriented psychotherapy is found particularly useful by some psychotherapists for a selected group of patients, often psychotic, but occasionally borderline, who present special problems with the elaboration and working through of the transference. Other psychotherapists routinely use dynamically oriented psychotherapy as their primary form of psychotherapy, both for patients who would benefit from a more analytically oriented approach and for those who would not. Although this form of psychotherapy includes supportive elements, it is based on helping the patient to understand aspects of herself that she is unaware of; the approach is thus considered "dynamic." This kind of psychotherapy typically focuses more on selective problem areas than does analytically oriented psychotherapy.

Supportive Psychotherapy

In supportive psychotherapy the patient comes for regularly scheduled sessions, usually once a week but sometimes more frequently, for varying but often lengthy periods. The principle underlying the number of sessions scheduled is virtually the opposite of that used in the more analytically oriented psychotherapies. In the latter approaches, increased sessions are used to promote intensity and regression. In supportive psychotherapy the goal is to stop regression, not to promote it. Here more frequent sessions are employed to stem untoward regression, at times when the patient is having acute difficulty with some of his basic ego functions. When the patient is doing "well," a lower frequency of sessions, usually once a week, generally suffices. In supportive psychotherapy contact between patient and therapist outside the sessions is promoted only to the extent that it is necessary to stem regression. Sessions are always conducted with the patient and therapist sitting across from each other. Instructions to the patient are simply to discuss those events in his life with which he is having difficulty.

Supportive psychotherapy is best suited for individuals with active disturbances in a number of their ego functions. This form of psychotherapy is indicated for a large group of basically psychotic individuals, although another large group of these psychotic patients can benefit more from dynamically oriented psychotherapy, at least some of the time. Supportive psychotherapy is also used by some in the treatment of selected borderline individuals. This form of psychotherapy is sometimes supplemented by psychiatric medication.

The purpose of supportive psychotherapy is to help build up the patient's weak ego functions—hence the often-used term *ego building*. For this purpose many types of therapeutic intervention are employed, including education, suggestion, clarification, reassurance, advice, and instruction, but not usually interpretation. For these interventions to be most successful, the maintenance of a positive transference and a working alliance is exceptionally important. For this reason, the transference is usually not discussed unless it is a resistance. Likewise, transference distortions are often rapidly corrected by education and reality testing. In supportive psychotherapy the therapist is often unable to maintain a neutral position, although she should strive to do so when possible. For this kind of psychotherapy to proceed optimally, free association is not wanted. What is wanted is a detailed description of the day-to-day events that led to the patient's current difficulty with his ego functions. Hence, contrary to the more analytically oriented approaches, the focus is on the here and now, and reporting of weekly events is encouraged.

The initial goal of supportive psychotherapy is to help the patient strengthen and maintain his ego functioning so that he can adapt adequately in day-to-day interactions. When the patient begins to function acceptably in this realm, further goals are added. A second and more difficult goal is to help the patient identify and accept those areas in which he is sensitive and vulnerable to regression. Once these areas are identified and accepted by the patient, he can then begin to learn to deal with them more effectively and gradually to respond to them by means other than regression. The tasks of helping the patient to identify these stressful areas and then to deal more effectively with them can be very time consuming. As this work is pursued, the psychotherapeutic approach often becomes more exploratory and often switches to a dynamically oriented framework. If and when the patient is able to make this switch, it is considered a welcome psychotherapeutic advance.

Generally, individuals will maximize their gains in psychotherapy by undergoing the most insight-oriented approach that they can tolerate. Thus, if an individual clearly meets the criteria for psychoanalysis, he can expect to gain much more from this approach than from analytically oriented psychotherapy. Likewise, if an individual can easily tolerate analytically oriented psychotherapy, he can expect to gain much more from that approach than from dynamically oriented psychotherapy. Analogously, a number of basically psychotic individuals can benefit more from dynamically oriented psychotherapy than from a more supportive approach, at least some of the time. If a patient is placed in a psychotherapy that he cannot tolerate, unnecessary regression can ensue. Careful evaluation in accordance with the ego psychological diagnostic approach will usually enable the therapist to match the patient with the optimal therapeutic approach. In those cases in which, after thorough scrutiny, there is still uncertainty, a careful trial of the psychotherapy that seems most suitable can be undertaken. If the chosen form of psychotherapy does not prove to be optimal, it can always be modified or changed.

CHAPTER 16

Psychotherapy with the Borderline Patient

All four of the different types of psychotherapies reviewed in the last chapter, in addition to a number of modifications and mixtures of the four approaches, have been used with some borderline patients. The treatment advocated reflects not only the therapist's theoretical persuasion and orientation, but also his definition of the term *borderline*. Thus, a number of psychoanalysts of the British school (Bion 1967, Rosenfeld 1965, Segal 1964) who employ psychoanalysis for basically psychotic individuals also use it for the borderline patient. Boyer and Giovacchini (1967) and Giovacchini (1978, 1984) also recommend psychoanalysis with few modifications for borderline patients. Abend, Porder, and Willick (1983) used classical psychoanalysis very effectively for their four relatively healthy borderline patients. Analogously, psychoanalysis might make sense for some of the healthier subgroups of Meissner's classification (1982-1983, 1983, 1984). Kernberg also allows for certain select borderline patients to be psychoanalyzed. At the other end of the continuum, Zetzel (1971) and Grinker (1975) use a purely supportive approach. Although many of the early psychoanalytic writers also recommended a supportive approach, the current consensus now seems to have shifted more to the use of modified analytically oriented psychotherapy. A number of these modified analytically oriented approaches have been described in the literature. These reports include the work of Kernberg (1968, 1975, 1976b, 1978, 1980a, 1982), Rinsley (1977, 1978), Masterson (1972, 1976, 1978) and Adler and Buie (Adler 1981, 1985, Adler and Buie 1979, Buie and Adler 1982–1983), among others. These approaches vary in detail, often in accordance with different underlying theoretical conceptualizations.

Of these approaches, that of Kernberg is possibly the most influential today. The work of Rinsley and Masterson and that of Adler and Buie is also highly recognized. All three of these psychotherapeutic approaches are modified versions of analytically oriented psychotherapy. Because they represent possibly the three most influential approaches to this type of psychotherapy, each will be succinctly summarized. The work of Abend, Porder, and Willick (1983) will be presented as an example of the application of psychoanalysis to some borderline patients. In contrast, the work of Zetzel (1971) will be presented as an example of a supportive approach.

Expressive Psychotherapy (Kernberg)

Kernberg (1968, 1975, 1976b, 1978, 1980a, 1982) has outlined a specific kind of psychoanalytically oriented psychotherapy, which he calls expressive psychotherapy, that he finds useful for many borderline patients. It is basically a modification of the pure form of analytically oriented psychotherapy we have described. The therapist's neutrality is maintained as much as possible, interpretation and clarification are the primary therapeutic techniques, and the main therapeutic focus is on the exploration of the transference. Because of the borderline's specific psychopathology, however, none of these three tasks can be carried out in exactly the same way as in either psychoanalysis or the pure form of analytically oriented psychotherapy. Primitive transferences become immediately active in the treatment setting and serve as resistances. These primitive transferences are based on multiple contradictory self and object images, include numerous primitive defenses, and can appear quite chaotic initially. They often result in severe acting out and psychotic distortions within the transference, which can undermine and threaten the overall treatment process. Accordingly, therapeutic focus on these transferences must be rapid and in the here and now. Interpretation and clarification remain the major techniques used to deal with the transferences, but these techniques are often not enough. Interventions involving the structuring of the external life of the patient are often needed. Time-limited hospitalization may become necessary. These interventions make it impossible for the therapist to remain neutral at all times, although the goal of returning to the neutral position whenever possible is maintained. Because of the need for intense focus on those areas in which acting out and reality distortions threaten the treatment, exploration of the transference is not as systematic as in psychoanalysis proper. With much psychotherapeutic work, the more primitive transferences are gradually worked through and replaced by more typically "neurotic" transferences. As this happens, the treatment becomes more similar to analytically oriented psychotherapy in the pure sense.

Noting the difficulties typically recurring when the borderline patient is treated using the expressive approach, Kernberg (1982) offers a number of guidelines in managing the transference. These guidelines are actually deviations from the usual techniques of analytically oriented psychotherapy. There is a basic strategy of interpretating the negative transference and the primitive aspects of the positive transference while "respecting" those aspects of the positive transference that gradually foster the development of the therapeutic alliance. Negative transferences are systematically elaborated initially only in the here and now, without psychogenetic reconstructions. Because interpretation of the primitive defenses gradually brings about structural change, thus strengthening the ego, the typical primitive defensive constellations are interpreted as soon as they enter the transference. The borderline patient often distorts the therapist's interpretations, so the patient's understanding of the therapist's interpretations must be regularly and systematically examined and clarified. As mentioned, because there is such a tendency for destructive acting out of the transference, limit setting and structuring of the patient's life outside of the therapy hours is often necessary. Such structuring sometimes includes the need for short-term hospitalization. As the patient advances in psychotherapy, the more primitive transferences are gradually converted to higher-level, or "neurotic," transferences. As this happens, these guidelines are needed less and less frequently, and the therapy evolves toward analytically oriented psychotherapy in the pure form.

Modified Exploratory Approach (Rinsley and Masterson)

Another influential psychotherapeutic strategy, also in the psychoanalytically oriented area, is that of Rinsley (1977, 1978) and Masterson (1972, 1976, 1978). These authors describe what they believe actually transpires in early childhood between the child and the parents to cause the child to enter the borderline state. The mother, often a borderline personality herself and deriving much gratification from the symbiotic involvement with the child, withdraws her emotional availability when the child begins to make an effort to separate and individuate, and confines her support to time when the child is passive, dependent, and compliant. This process peaks at the rapprochement subphase (16 to 25 months of age) of the separation–individuation period. In accordance with this maternal behavior, the child internalizes what Rinsley and Masterson have termed the split object relations unit. This split object relations unit is composed of two part units, each consisting of three parts, as detailed in Chapter 10. The persistence of this split object relations unit leads to the psychopathology associated with the borderline personality.

The psychotherapeutic strategy of Rinsley and Masterson involves the activation, elaboration, and working through of the split object relations unit within the transference. The borderline patient starts therapy with the rewarding part unit being ego syntonic and with little awareness of the psychological cost of this. The rewarding part unit is expressed in the general ego-syntonic borderline psychopathology, which came about because of the persistence of this part unit. From the outset the therapist begins a process of confrontations and clarifications to demonstrate to the patient the self-destructive nature of this part unit. By this process the rewarding part unit becomes progressively ego dystonic, and there is an activation of the withdrawing part unit. The withdrawing part unit, however, will be resisted, with the reemergence of the rewarding part unit. A kind of circular process goes on, with continual confrontation and clarification of the destructiveness of the rewarding part unit, the emergence of the withdrawing part unit, resistance to this emergence, the reemergence of the rewarding part unit, a repeat of the confrontation and clarification, and so forth.

With time, a new alliance between therapist and patient develops to help render the rewarding part unit ego dystonic. This is an alliance, built up as the patient internalizes the therapist as a positive external object, between the therapist's healthy ego and the "embattled-reality ego" of the patient. This alliance produces a new "healthy" object relations unit for the patient, as follows:

a. Representation of therapist: supportive and approving when patient strives for appropriate growth
b. Representation of self: capable, developing, good
c. Affect: feeling good, gratified

The activation of this new healthy object relations unit, in combination with the repetitive confrontations, clarifications, and, later, interpretations involving the split object relations unit, allows the patient gradually to become aware of the part units within himself and work these through. Via the working-through process, the part units become integrated and the healthy object relations unit becomes predominant. The working-through process includes efforts at understanding the childhood determinants of the split object relations unit and thus the cause of the psychopathology. The latter psychotherapeutic work is thought to include elements of "classical" analysis in an attempt to uncover these unconscious childhood determinants.

This summary is an oversimplification of the technical aspects of the psychotherapeutic work of Rinsley and Masterson. The type of therapy involved is called a "modified exploratory approach," and, like Kernberg's approach, it can be classified as a kind of modified psychoanalytically oriented psychotherapy. In accordance with Kernberg's recommendations, the therapist's neutrality is maintained, confrontation, clarification, and interpretation (later) are the primary therapeutic techniques, and the main therapeutic focus is on the exploration of the transference. Primitive transferences, based on all good and all bad object relations units, become immediately active in the treatment setting. It is the working through and resolution of these transferences that is the crucial aspect of the psychotherapy. With much psychotherapeutic work, the more primitive transferences are replaced by higher-level transferences. Thus the psychotherapeutic process of Rinsley and Masterson, in broad outline, is similar to that of Kernberg. It differs from Kernberg's in its specificity. Rinsley and Masterson's theory of the causes of the borderline personality is very specific, and the psychotherapeutic techniques recommended are equally specific. Kernberg (1982) considers Rinsley and Masterson to be describing work with what he calls infantile personalities, a subgroup of his borderline personality category.

Phase-specific Treatment (Adler and Buie)

Adler and Buie (Adler 1981, 1985, Adler and Buie 1979, Buie and Adler 1982–1983) have introduced a psychotherapeutic approach that also is a modified version of analytically oriented psychotherapy. They hypothesize a deficit in a specific kind of introject, the holding introject, as central to the borderline psychopathology. The lack of holding introjects in the borderline personality arises because of the absence of good-enough mothering in the phases of separation–individuation. In the face of this lack, the individual must depend in an ongoing way on external objects, or self-objects, to provide the needed holding and soothing. The holding self-object is crucial in providing essential holding and soothing for the borderline individual; it is needed for the maintenance of psychological integrity. Disturbances in the holding self-object can lead to rage, regression, separation anxiety, aloneness, and annihilation anxiety.

Psychotherapy with the borderline patient must first address the core deficit, the lack of the holding introjects. Adler and Buie describe three successive phases of treatment in dealing with the borderline's core deficit. The aim of Phase I is to establish and maintain a relationship in which the therapist can be used as a holding self-object. When this goal is attained, the patient is able to develop insight into the nature of his aloneness and to acquire a stable memory of the therapist as a sustaining holder. Subsequently the memory can serve as a substrate out of which holding introjects can be formed. The formation of holding introjects completes the work of Phase I.

During Phase I, in which the patient–therapist relationship substitutes for and corrects the original developmental failure in good-enough mothering, a number of impediments to the use of the therapist as a holding self-object emerge. Because of the tenuous nature of the developing self-object, aloneness is activated in the transference, with the concomitant emergence of rage, attempts at incorporation and fusion, and associated primitive guilt. The major focus of Phase I is the working through of these impediments in the transference, by repetitive clarifications, confrontations, and interpretations. Although this approach is basically insight oriented, the treatment must be conducted in a supportive way, to help maintain the evolving tenuous holding introjects and to help avoid intense separation anxiety and annihilation anxiety. The therapist must do everything possible to act as a holding self-object in reality. Techniques to sustain this role, such as extra appointments, telephone calls, and rigorous clarifications of the reality of the therapist's existence as a holding object, must be brought into play. If regression is severe, brief hospitalizations may be required. Over time the patient learns that the therapist is an enduring, reliable, and good holding self-object. Via working through, insight, and internalization, the patient is able to convert this holding self-object into a holding introject.

Phase I ends when holding introjects are fairly firmly established. The problem is that the initial holding introjects are considerably unrealistic and highly idealized, patterned after qualities of whatever positive introjects were formed in the early years. The aim of Phase II is to convert these unrealistic idealized holding introjects into more realistic, mature holding introjects. Adler and Buie model their work after that of Kohut in this phase. By a process of "optimal disillusionment," in which the patient gradually notices differences between the idealized holding introjects and the actual holding qualities of the therapist, work in this phase takes place with little direct intervention needed. Ultimately the holding introjects are modified in accordance with reality.

Because most of Adler and Buie's borderline patients also exhibit serious narcissistic pathology, as described by Kohut and elaborated on in Chapter 12, Phase II addresses these problems as well. As the idealized holding introjects are modified in accordance with reality, so also are the narcissistic introjects modified. As Phase II evolves, the borderline patient begins to look much like the narcissistic patient of Kohut; accordingly, psychotherapeutic work proceeds in accordance with Kohut's recommendations. Adler and Buie believe that work with the pathological narcissicism cannot be undertaken until holding introjects are adequately stable. Thus, Phase II must be relatively advanced in this regard before definitive work with the narcissism can take place.

The aim of Phase III is to convert the holding introjects into more definitive psychic structures. By the end of this phase, a rather mature ego and superego should be established. Specifically, the ego should have the capacity for pleasurable confidence in the self and for directing affectionate love toward the self. Correspondingly, the superego must no longer be harsh and must serve as a source of a realistically deserved sense of worth. The work of Phase III continues along the lines of Kohut's conceptualizations, with internalization processes, termed *transmuting internalizations* by Kohut, playing a major role. Various kinds of subtle self-object functions continue to be necessary to provide the experiences out of which the patient can, via identification, develop his own autonomous capacities. These capacities include the ability to be held and soothed on one's own, the feeling of the reality of one's own self-worth and competence, and the ability to be affectionately loving to oneself. At the end of this phase, the patient has acquired genuine psychological stability, varying in degree from patient to patient.

Adler and Buie believe that the important elements of their psychotherapeutic approach are analytical. Basically, the therapist's neutrality is maintained, confrontation, clarification, and interpretation are primary therapeutic techniques, and the main therapeutic focus is on the exploration of the transference. Techniques involving the use of the therapist as a self-object are required extensively, however, and the reliance on these techniques makes this form of psychotherapy less analytical. Nevertheless, Adler and Buie's approach does seem to qualify as a modified kind of psychoanalytically oriented psychotherapy.

The focus on the deficiency of holding introjects, unique to this form of psychotherapy, seems of clear clinical value for a number of borderline patients. The view that Adler and Buie's borderline patients, when approximately in Phase II, become very similar to Kohut's narcissistic personalities and do best with psychotherapeutic techniques advocated by Kohut seems more questionable.

Classical Psychoanalysis (Abend, Porder, and Willick)

Abend, Porder, and Willick (1983) used unmodified "classical" psychoanalysis for the treatment of their four borderline patients. Although they caution against generalization, they clearly believe that psychoanalysis is indicated for at least some borderline individuals. The patients of Abend and co-workers, although representing a group of patients with severe psychopathology, are nevertheless clearly healthier than the group deemed borderline by the ego psychological approach emphasized in this book. The successful use of psychoanalysis in the four patients is noteworthy in itself. When comparing the approach used with other approaches, however, the degree of psychopathology of the four patients must be considered. In contrast to Abend and colleagues, those of the British school (Bion 1967, Rosenfeld 1965, Segal 1964) employ psychoanalysis for basically any borderline individual, along with many psychotic individuals as well. The techniques used by this British school, however, contrast greatly with the classical psychoanalysis used by Abend, Porder, and Willick. The techniques of Abend, Porder, and Willick correspond to those described in the section on psychoanalysis in Chapter 15 of this book.

Although they employed no special techniques with four patients, Abend and colleagues did believe that the psychoanalysis of these four individuals was in some ways different from that of the usual neurotic. In particular, there was the need to interpret and reinterpret projection mechanisms carefully. There was the need to pay attention constantly to any partial failures in reality testing. Sadomasochistic conflicts, acting out, and the pervasiveness of transference distortions demanded special attention. Change took place very slowly and intermittently, and discouragement within the analyst was frequent.

Abend and co-workers expressed disagreement with Kernberg, Rinsley, and Masterson in certain areas. The former group saw little value in confronting the patient's contradictory attitudes during assessment interviews. They disagreed with the selective focus on the negative transference, and took issue with emphasizing aggressive over libidinal conflicts. They disagreed with the suggestion of avoiding genetic interpretations early in the treatment, believing that these interpretations, when possible, were very helpful. They found the material forthcoming in the opening phases of treatment to be extremely confusing and obscure, and were unable to see the primitive transferences described by others until much later in the treatment. They did not conceptualize the conflicts that emerged in treatment as coming from specific developmental times, such as the rapprochement subphase of the separation–individuation period; instead, they were impressed by the extent to which the material of their patients reflected concerns from various developmental periods. They did not advocate understanding and interpreting material in any preplanned manner. Instead, their basic therapeutic approach was similar to that used with healthier patients. No special techniques were held to be needed or recommended.

Although Abend and co-workers disagree with Kernberg on a number of issues, the differences between the two approaches may simply stem from the differences in psychopathology of the respective patients. Kernberg might be very willing to start with an open-ended, analytically oriented approach and make modifications only when necessary. If the patients of Abend and co-workers were in treatment with Kernberg, Kernberg might offer no more modifications than these workers did and end up doing psychoanalysis. Correspondingly, if Abend and colleagues were to treat some of Kernberg's more difficult borderline patients, they might find it useful and necessary to make modifications in technique analogous to those suggested by Kernberg.

Supportive Psychotherapy (Zetzel)

Zetzel (1971) believes that there are three developmental steps in the attainment of definitive psychic structure, all initiated in the early mother–child relationship. The first is the achievement of definitive self-object differentiation. The second is the capacity to recognize, tolerate, and master separation, loss, and narcissistic injury. The third is the internalization of an ego identification and self-esteem that will permit autonomy and the capacity to maintain stable one-to-one relationships. The borderline individual displays some difficulty with all three steps. There is only a relative failure in achieving the first step, most often expressed under stress and usually readily reversible. Regarding the second step, there is again a relative but this time a more significant failure, but one that can be considerably alleviated with psychotherapy. The borderline individual has only limited capabilities for achieving the third step, and for this reason, many such patients are relatively interminable in psychotherapy.

Zetzel believes that intensive psychotherapy can present dangers to patients who suffer from these developmental failures. She holds that these patients tend to regress too much during intensive psychotherapy, tend to blur reality and transference, and are intolerant of painful affects associated with regressive transferences. Therefore, regressions are to be avoided, and instead focus should be on progression and mastery. Zetzel's psychotherapeutic technique is based on the necessity for developing and maintaining a stable, realistic, and consistent patient–therapist relationship. She posits that regular but limited contact (seldom more than once a week) is optimal in maintaining a good working relationship. Improvement is best achieved by the establishment of a new and better relationship than had been attained during early development, a relationship based on a working alliance and involving minimal transference. During psychotherapy meetings considerable activity and structure are used to focus actively on the patient's problems. Zetzel believes that this type of psychotherapy can help certain borderline patients maintain a high degree of adaptation, as long as the therapist remains available to the patient for an unlimited period of time.

Zetzel's type of psychotherapy is a more supportive approach than the others described. Although it does enable the borderline patient to correct some of his deficiencies, it accepts other deficits as a kind of given and tries to help the patient to adapt to his limitations as well as possible. This type of psychotherapy combines elements of dynamically oriented psychotherapy and supportive psychotherapy as described in Chapter 15. The approach is not currently in vogue, because the consensus has shifted toward the use of more analytically oriented psychotherapies for the borderline patient. Nevertheless, supportive forms of psychotherapy probably continue to be the approaches most widely used in dealing with borderline individuals.

Concluding Comments

Five contrasting methods of psychotherapy for borderline individuals have been presented in this chapter. The different

methods in part correspond to different theoretical orienta-
tions regarding the borderline patient, different definitions of
the term *borderline*, and different levels of optimism regarding
eventual psychotherapeutic outcome. Presently it is difficult to
compare one method with another on eventual outcome. As
has already been emphasized, the borderline group consists of
a great variety of widely different individuals. One method of
psychotherapy may be clearly applicable and useful for one
individual, whereas another method may be better for a second
patient.

Learning how to perform effective psychotherapy with
borderline patients is somewhat equivalent to learning how to
perform effective psychotherapy in general. The patient must
be thoroughly evaluated initially, to determine first whether he
is a borderline personality and then what psychotherapeutic
approach will be of most help. The ego psychological diagnostic approach is invaluable for this purpose. Highlighting
the patient's ego strengths and ego weaknesses permits ten-
tative conclusions to be reached about the necessary areas and
techniques of psychotherapeutic intervention. When the actual
psychotherapy begins, it must be initiated cautiously, with the
therapist constantly evaluating whether the modality of treatment chosen is optimal for the patient. The therapist retains the
flexibility of either modifying her basic approach or switching
to an approach more in accordance with the patient's needs.
Despite Zetzel's work, it appears that it is therapeutically
optimal for the patient to undergo the most insight-oriented
approach that can be tolerated. Caution must always be
exercised when actually changing to a more insight-oriented
approach, however, to be certain that the patient can indeed
tolerate the approach without untoward regression.

REFERENCES

Abend, S., Porder, M., and Willick, M. (1983). *Borderline Patients: Psychoanalytic Perspectives*. New York: International Universities Press.

Adler, G. (1981). The borderline–narcissistic personality disorder continuum. *American Journal of Psychiatry* 138:46–50.

_____ (1985). *Borderline Psychopathology and Its Treatment*. New York: Jason Aronson.

Adler, G., and Buie, D. (1979). Aloneness and borderline psychopathology: the possible relevance of child development issues. *International Journal of Psychoanalysis* 60:83–96.

Akhtar, S., and Thomson, J. (1982). Overview: narcissistic personality disorder. *American Journal of Psychiatry* 139:12–20.

Akiskal, H. (1981). Subaffective disorders: dysthymic, cyclothymic and bipolar II disorders in the borderline realm. In *The Psychiatric Clinics of North America, Symposium on Borderline Disorders*. Philadelphia: Saunders.

American Psychiatric Association (1952). *Diagnostic and Statistical Manual of Mental Disorders*. Washington, D. C.: American Psychiatric Association.

_____ (1968). *Diagnostic and Statistical Manual of Mental*

Disorders. 2nd ed. Washington, D. C.: American Psychiatric Association.

———— (1980). *Diagnostic and Statistical Manual of Mental Disorders.* 3rd ed. Washington, D. C.: American Psychiatric Association.

Andrulonis, R. A., Gloeck, B. C., Stroebel, C. F., Vogel, N.G., Shapiro, A. L., and Aldridge, D. M. (1981). Organic brain dysfunction and the borderline syndrome. In *The Psychiatric Clinics of North America,* ed. M. H. Stone. Philadelphia: Saunders.

Arieti, S. (1955). *Interpretation of Schizophrenia,* pp. 194-202. New York: Robert Brunner.

Astrachan, B., Harrow, M., Adler, D., Baver, L., Schwartz, A., Schwartz, C., and Tucker, G. *et al.* (1972). A checklist for the diagnosis of schizophrenia. *British Journal of Psychiatry* 121: 529-539.

Bak, R. (1954). The schizophrenic defense against aggression. *International Journal of Psychoanalysis* 35:129.

Bellak, L. (1958). *Schizophrenia: A Review of the Syndrome,* pp. 3-34. New York: Logos Press.

———— (1970). The validity and usefulness of the concept of the schizophrenic syndrome. In *The Schizophrenic Reaction,* ed. B. Cancro, pp. 41-58. New York: Brunner/Mazel.

Bellak, L., Hurvich, M., and Gediman, H. (1973). *Ego Functions in Schizophrenics, Neurotics, and Normals: A Systematic Study of Conceptual, Diagnostic, and Therapeutic Aspects.* New York: Wiley.

Bellak, L., and Meyers, B. (1975). Ego function assessment and analysability. *International Review of Psychoanalysis* 2:413-427.

Beres, D. (1956). Ego deviation and the concept of schizophrenia. In *The Psychoanalytic Study of the Child,* vol. 2, pp. 164-235. New York: International Universities Press.

Bibring, E. (1954). Psychoanalysis and the dynamic psychotherapies. *Journal of the American Psychoanalytic Association* 2:745-770.

Bion, W. (1967). *Second Thoughts: Selected Papers on Psychoanalysis.* New York: Basic Books.

Bleuler, E. (1950). *Dementia Praecox or the Group of Schizophrenia* (German, 1911). New York: International Universities Press.

Boesky, D. (1983). The problem of mental representation in self and object theory. *Psychoanalytic Quarterly* 52:564–583.

Boyer, L., and Giovacchini, P. (1967). *Psychoanalytic Treatment of Characterological and Schizophrenic Disorders*. New York: Jason Aronson.

Brenner, C. (1955). *An Elementary Textbook of Psychoanalysis*. New York: International Universities Press.

Buie, D., and Adler, G. (1982–1983). Definitive treatment of the borderline personality. *International Journal of Psychoanalytic Psychotherapy* 9:51–87.

Bychowsky, G. (1953). The problem of latent psychosis. *Journal of the American Psychoanalytic Association* 4:484–503.

Carpenter, W., and Strauss, J. (1973). Flexible system for the diagnosis of schizophrenia: Report from the WHO International Pilot Study for Schizophrenia. *Science* 182:1275–1278.

Carr, C., Goldstein, E., Hunt, H., and Kernberg, O. (1979). Psychological tests and borderline patients. *Journal of Personality Assessment* 43:582–590.

Cooper, J., Kendell, R., Gurland, B., Sharpe, L., Copeland, J., and Simon, R. *et al.* (1972). *Psychiatric Diagnosis in New York and London*. Maudsley Monographs, no. 20. London: Oxford University Press.

Deutsch, H. (1942). Some forms of emotional disturbance and their relation to schizophrenia. *Psychoanalytic Quarterly* 11:301–321.

Dewald, P. (1971). *Psychotherapy: A Dynamic Approach*. New York: Basic Books.

Dunaif, S., and Hoch, P. (1955). Pseudopsychopathic schizophrenia. In *Psychiatry and the Law*, eds. P. Hoch and J. Zubin. New York: Grune & Stratton.

Erikson, E. (1956). The problem of ego identity. *Journal of the American Psychoanalytic Association* 4:56-121.

Federn, P. (1952). *Ego Psychology and the Psychoses*, pp. 184-196. New York: Basic Books.

Feighner, J., Robins, E., Guze, S., Woodruff, R., Winohur, G., and Munoz, R., *et al.* (1972). Diagnostic criteria for use in psychiatric research. *Archives of General Psychiatry* 26:57-63.

Fenton, W., Mosher, L., and Matthews, S. (1981). Diagnosis of schizophrenia: a critical review of current diagnostic systems. *Schizophrenia Bulletin* 7:452-476.

Freud, A. (1936). *The Ego and the Mechanisms of Defense*. New York: International Universities Press.

Freud, S. (1911) Psychoanalytic notes on an autobiographical account of a case of paranoia. *Standard Edition* 12:3-82.

_____ (1914). On narcissism: an introduction. *Standard Edition* 14:67-102.

_____ (1923). The ego and the id. *Standard Edition* 19:3-66

_____ (1940). An outline of psychoanalysis. *Standard Edition* 23:144-207.

Frosch, J. (1964). The psychotic character: clinical psychiatric considerations. *Psychiatric Quarterly* 38:81-96.

_____ (1970). Psychoanalytic considerations of the psychotic character. *Journal of the American Psychoanalytic Association* 18:24-50.

Gill, M. (1954). Psychoanalysis and exploratory psychotherapy. *Journal of the American Psychoanalytic Association* 2:771-797.

Giovacchini, P. (1978). The psychoanalytic treatment of the alienated patient. In *New Perspectives on Psychotherapy of the Borderline Adult*, ed. J. F. Masterson, pp. 3-19. New York: Brunner/Mazel.

_____ (1984). *Character Disorders and Adaptive Mechanisms*. New York: Jason Aronson.

Gitelson, M. (1958). On ego distortions. *International Journal of Psychoanalysis* 39:243-257.

Goldstein, W. (1979). The diagnosis of schizophrenia. *Psychiatric Annals* 9 (12):15–27.

_____ (1981a). A study of impulse control in the borderline patient. *Psychiatria Clinica* 14:81–87.

_____ (1981b). The borderline personality. *Psychiatric Annals* 11:22–26.

_____ (1982). Understanding Kernberg on the borderline patient. *Journal: National Association of Private Psychiatric Hospitals* 13 (1): 21–26.

_____ (1983). *DSM-III* and the diagnosis of borderline. *American Journal of Psychotherapy* 37: 312–327.

_____ (1984). Confirmation of the borderline personality within a psychodynamic framework. *Psychopathology: International Journal of Descriptive Psychopathology and Clinical Diagnostics.* 17: 59–66.

_____ (1985a). *DMS-III* and the Narcissistic Personality. American Journal of Psychotherapy 39, 1:4–16.

_____ (1985c). A succinct overview of psychotherapy, submitted for publication.

_____ (1985b) Kernberg on the borderline: a simplified version, submitted for publication.

Gottesman, I., and Shields, J. (1972). *Schizophrenia and Genetics: A Twin Study Vantage Point.* New York: Academic Press.

Grinker, R. (1975). Neurosis, psychosis, and borderline states. In *Comprehensive Textbook of Psychiatry*, eds. A. Freedman, H. Kaplan, and B. Sadoch. Baltimore: Williams & Wilkins.

Grinker, R., Werble, B., and Drye, R. (1968). *The Borderline Syndrome.* New York: Basic Books.

Grotstein, J. (1977a). The psychoanalytic concept of schizophrenia. I. The dilemma. *International Journal of Psychoanalysis* 58: 403–425.

_____ (1977b). The Psychoanalytic concept of schizophrenia. II. Reconciliation. *International Journal of Pschoanalysis* 58: 427–452.

Gunderson, J. (1977). Characteristics of borderlines. In *Borderline Personality Disorders: The Concept, the Syndrome, the Patient*, ed. P. Hartocollis. New York: International Universities Press.

_____ (1982). Empirical studies of the borderline diagnosis. In *Psychiatry 1982*, ed. L. Grinspoon. Washington, D. C.: American Psychiatric Press.

_____ (1984). *Borderline Personality Disorder*. Washington, D.C.: American Psychiatric Press.

Gunderson, J., Carpenter, W., and Strauss, J. (1975). Borderline and schizophrenic patients: a comparative study. *American Journal of Psychiatry* 132:1257.

Gunderson, J., and Kolb, J. (1978). Discriminating features of borderline patients. *American Journal of Psychiatry* 135: 792–796.

Gunderson, J., Kolb, J., and Austin, V. (1981). The diagnostic interveiw for borderlines (DIB). *American Journal of Psychiatry* 138:896.

Gunderson, J., Siever, L., and Spaulding, E. (1983). The search for a schizotype. *Archives of General Psychiatry* 40:15.

Gunderson, J., and Singer, M. (1975). Defining borderline patients: an overview. *American Journal of Psychiatry* 132: 1–10.

Hartmann, H. (1939). *Ego Psychology and the Problem of Adaptation*. New York: International Universities Press, 1958.

_____ (1953). Contribution to the metapsychology of schizophrenia. In *The Psychoanalytic Study of the Child*, vol. 8. New York: International Universities Press.

_____ (1955). Notes on the theory of sublimation. *Journal of the American Psychoanalytic Association* 10: 9–29.

Hartmann, H., Kris, E., and Lowenstein, R. (1946). Comments on the formation of psychic structure. In *The Psychoanalytic Study of the Child*, vol. 2. New York: International Universities Press.

Hoch, P., and Cattell, J. (1959). The diagnosis of pseudoneurotic schizophrenia. *Psychoanalytic Quarterly* 23: 17–43.

Hoch, P., and Polatin, P. (1949). Pseudoneurotic forms of schizophrenia. *Psychoanalytic Quarterly* 23: 248–276.

Jacobson, E. (1964). *The Self and the Object World*. New York: International Universities Press.

Kernberg, O. (1966). Structural derivatives of object relations. *International Journal of Psychoanalysis* 47: 236-253.

_____ (1967). Borderline personality organization. *Journal of the American Psychoanalytic Association* 15: 641-685.

_____ (1968). The treatment of patients with borderline personality organization. *International Journal of Psychoanalysis* 49: 600-619.

_____ (1970). Factors in the treatment of narcissistic personality disorder. *Journal of the American Psychoanalytic Association* 18: 51-85.

_____ (1971). A psychoanalytic classification of character pathology. *Journal of the American Psychoanalytic Association* 18: 800-821.

_____ (1974). Further contributions to the treatment of narcissistic personalities. *International Journal of Psychoanalysis* 55: 215-240.

_____ (1975). *Borderline Conditions and Pathological Narcissism*. New York: Jason Aronson.

_____ (1976a). *Object Relations Theory and Clinical Psycoanalysis*. New York: Jason Aronson.

_____ (1976b). Technical considerations in the treatment of borderline personality organization. *Journal of the American Psychoanalytic Association* 24: 795-829.

_____ (1977). Structural diagnosis of borderline personality organization. In *Borderline Personality Disorders: The Concept, the Syndrome, the Patient*, ed. P. Hartocollis. pp. 87-123. New York: International Universities Press.

_____ (1978). Contrasting approaches to the psychotherapy of borderline conditions. In *New Perspectives of Psychotherapy of the Borderline Adult*, ed. J. F. Masterson, pp. 77-104. New York: Brunner/Mazel.

_____ (1980a). *Internal World and External Reality*. New York: Jason Aronson.

———(1980b). Neurosis, psychosis, and borderline states. In *Comprehensive Textbook of Psychiatry*, vol. 3, 3rd ed., eds. A. Freedman, H. Kaplan, and B. Sadoch. Baltimore: Williams & Wilkins.

——— (1981). Structural interviewing. In *The Psychiatric Clinics of North America, Symposium on Borderline Disorders*. Philadelphia: Saunders.

——— (1982). The psychotherapeutic treatment of borderline personalities. In *Psychiatry 1982: The American Psychiatric Association Annual Review*, ed. L. Grinspoon, pp. 470–487. Washington, D. C.: American Psychiatric Press.

——— (1984). Projection and Projective Identification: Development and Clinical Aspects. Paper presented at the Fall Meeting of the American Psychoanalytic Association, New York, December.

Kernberg, O., Goldstein, E., Carr, A., Hunt, H., Bauer, S., and Blumenthal, R. (1981). Diagnosing borderline personality: a pilot study using multiple diagnostic methods. *Journal of Nervous and Mental Disease* 169: 225–231.

Kety, S., Rosenthal, D., Wender, P., and Schulsinger, F. (1968). The types and prevalence of mental illness in the biological and adoptive families of adopted schizophrenics. In *The Transmission of Schizophrenia*, eds. D. Rosenthal and S. Kety. Oxford: Pergamon Press.

Kety, S., Rosenthal, D., Wender, P., Schulsinger, F., and Jacobsen, B., *et al.* (1975). Mental illness in the biological and adoptive families of adopted individuals who have become schizophrenics: a preliminary report based on psychiatric interviews. In *Genetic Research in Psychiatry*, eds. R. Fieve, D. Rosenthal, and H. Brill. New York: John Hopkins University Press.

Klein, D. (1977). Psychopharmocological treatment and delineation of borderline disorders. In *Borderline Personality Disorders: The Concept, the Syndrome, the Patient*, ed. P. Hartocollis. New York: International University Press.

Klein, M. (1946). Notes on some schizoid mechanisms. *International Journal of Psychoanalysis* 27:99.

Knight, R. (1953). Borderline states. *Bulletin of the Menninger Clinic* 17:1-12.

Kohut, H. (1966). Forms and transformations of narcissism. *Journal of the American Psychoanalytic Association* 14: 243-272.

_____ (1968). The psychoanalytic treatment of narcissistic personality disorders. *Psychoanalytic study of the Child* 23: 86-113.

_____ (1971). *The Analysis of the Self*. New York: International Universities Press.

_____ (1972). Thoughts on narcissism and narcissistic rage. *Psychoanalytic Study of the Child* 27:360-400.

_____ (1977). *The Restoration of the Self*. New York: International Universities Press.

Kohut, H., and Wolf, E. (1978). The disorders of the self and their treatment: an outline. *International Journal of Psychoanalysis* 59: 413-425.

Kraepelin, E. (1896). *Psychiatrie, Ein Lehrbuch fur Studierende and Arzte*. Leipzig: Barth.

Kris, E. (1952). *Psychoanalytic Explorations in Art*. New York: International Universities Press.

Kris, E., Lichtenberg, J., and Slap, J. (1973). Notes on the concept of splitting and the defense mechanism of splitting of representations. *Journal of the American Psychoanalytic Association*. 21: 772-787.

Mahler, M. (1970). *On Human Symbiosis and the Vicissitudes of Individuation*, vol. I, pp. 32-36. International Universities Press.

_____ (1971). A study of the separation-individuation process and its possible application to borderline phenomena in the psychoanalytic situation. In *The Psychoanalytic Study of the Child*, vol. 26, pp. 403-424. New York: Quadrangle.

Mahler, M., Pine, F., and Bergman, A. (1975). *The Psychological Birth of the Human Infant*. New York: Basic Books.

Masterson, J. (1972). *Treatment of the Borderline Adolescent: A Developmental Approach*. New York: Wiley-Interscience.

———— (1976). *Psychotherapy of the Borderline Adult: A Developmental Approach:* New York: Brunner/Mazel.

———— (1978). *New Perspectives on Psychotherapy of the Borderline Adult.* New York: Brunner/Mazel.

McDevitt, J. (1975). Separation–individuation and object constancy. *Journal of the American Psychoanalytic Association* 23: 713–742.

Meissner, W. (1978a). Notes on some conceptual aspects of the borderline personality organization. *International Review of Psychoanalysis* 5: 293–311.

———— (1978b). Theoretical assumptions of the concept of the borderline personality. *Journal of the American Psychoanalytic Association* 26: 559–598.

———— (1980). A note on projective identification. *Journal of the American Psychoanalytic Association* 28: 43–67.

———— (1981). Genetic aspects of the borderline conditions. *Psychoanalytic Review* 66: 219–241.

———— (1982–1983). Notes on the potential differentiation of borderline conditions. *International Journal of Psychoanalytic Psychotherapy* 9: 3–49.

———— (1983). Notes on the levels of differentiation within borderline conditions. *Psychoanalytic Review* 70:179–209.

———— (1984). *The Borderline Spectrum: Differential Diagnosis and Developmental Issues.* New York: Jason Aronson.

Ogden, T. (1979). On projective identification. *International Journal of Psychoanalysis* 670: 357–372.

Oppenheimer, H. (1971). *Clinical Psychiatry: Issues and Challenges,* pp. 227–246. New York: Harper & Row.

Overall, J., and Hollister, L. (1979). Comparative evaluation of research diagnostic criteria for schizophrenia. *Archives of General Psychiatry* 36: 1198–1205.

Perry, J., and Klerman, G. (1978). The borderline patient. *Archives of General Psychiatry* 35: 141–150.

———— (1980). Clinical features of the borderline personality. *American Journal of Psychiatry* 137: 165–173.

Piaget, J. (1954). *The Construction of Reality in the Child.* New York: Basic Books.

Pope, H., Jonas, J., Hudson, J., Cohen, B., and Gunderson J. *et al* (1983). The validity of *DSM-III* borderline personality disorder. *Archives of General Psychiatry* 40: 23.

Pope, H., and Lipinski, J. (1978). Diagnosis in schizophrenia and manic depressive illness. *Archives of General Psychiatry* 35: 811.

Pope, H., Lipinski, J., Cohen, B., and Axelrod, D. *et al.* (1980) Schizoaffective disorder": an invalid diagnosis? A comparison of schizoaffective disorder, schizophrenia, and affective disorders. *American Journal of Psychiatry* 137: 921.

Procci, W. (1976). Schizo-affective psychosis: fact or fiction? *Archives of General Psychiatry* 33: 1167.

Rapaport, D., Gill, M., and Schafer, R. (1945–1946). *Diagnostic Psychological Testing.* Chicago: Year Book.

Rinsley, D. (1977). An object relations view of the borderline personality. In *Borderline Personality Disorders: The Concept, the Syndrome, the Patient,* ed. P. Hartocollis. New York: International Universities Press.

———— (1978). Borderline psychopathology: a review of etiology, dynamics, and treatment. *International Review of Psychoanalysis* 5: 45.

Rosenfeld, H. (1965). *Psychotic States: A Psychoanalytical Approach.* New York: International Universities Press.

Rothstein, A. (1979). An exploration of the diagnostic term "narcissistic personality disorder." *Journal of the American Psychoanalytic Association* 27: 893–912.

Sandler, J., and Rosenblatt, B. (1962). The concept of the representational world. *Psychoanalytic Study of the Child* 17: 128–145.

Sartorius, N. (1973). Diagnosis and distribution of schizophrenia. In *WHO International Pilot Study of Schizophrenia,* vol. 1, pp. 14–17. Albany, N.Y.: World Health Organization.

Schneider, K. (1959). *Clinical Psychopathology.* Trans. M. Hamilton. New York: Grune & Stratton.

Segal, H. (1964). *Introduction to the Work of Melanie Klein.* New York: Basic Books.

Spitz, R. (1965). *The First Year of Life: A Psychoanalytic Study of*

Normal and Deviant Development of Object Relations. New York: International Universities Press.

Spitzer, R., Endicott, J., and Robins, E. (1978). Research diagnostic criteria: rationale and reliability. *Archives of General Psychiatry* 35: 773–782.

Spitzer, R., Endicott, J., and Gibbon, M. (1979). Crossing the border into borderline personality and borderline schizophrenia. *Archives of General Psychiatry* 36: 17.

Stern, A. (1938). Psychoanalytic investigation and therapy in the borderline group of neurosis. *Psychoanalytic Quarterly* 7: 467.

Stone, L. (1951). Psychoanalysis and brief psychotherapy. *Psychoanalytic Quarterly* 20: 215–236.

———— (1954). The widening scope of indications for psychoanalysis. *Journal of the American Psychoanalytic Association* 2: 567–594.

Stone, M. (1977). The borderline syndrome: evolution of the term, genetic aspects and prognosis. *American Journal of Psychotherapy* 31: 345.

Tarachow, S. (1963). *An Introduction to Psychotherapy.* New York: International Universities Press.

Ticho, E. (1970). Differences between psychoanalysis and psychotherapy. *Bulletin of the Menninger Clinic* 34: 128–139.

Vaillant, G. (1971). Theoretical hierarchy of adaptive ego mechanisms. *Psychiatry* 24: 107–118.

Wallerstein, R. (1965). The goals of psychoanalysis: a survey of analytic viewpoints. In *Psychotherapy and Psychoanalysis: Theory-Practice-Research,* pp. 99–118. New York: International Universities Press, 1975.

Winnicott, D. (1953). Transitional objects and transitional phenomena. In *Collected Papers,* pp. 229–242. London: Tavistock, 1958.

———— (1965). Ego distortion in terms of the true and false self. In *The Maturation Processes and the Facilitating Environment,* pp.140-152. New York: International Universities Press.

_____ (1969). The use of an object. *International Journal of Psychoanalysis* 50: 711–716.

Wurmser, L. (1974). Psychoanalytic considerations of the etilogy of compulsive drug use. *Journal of the American Psychoanalytic Association* 22: 820–843.

Zetzel, E. (1968). The so-called good hysteric. *International Journal of Psychoanalysis* 49: 256–260.

_____ (1971). A developmental approach to the borderline patient. *American Journal of Psychiatry* 127: 867–871.

Zilboorg, G. (1941). Ambulatory schizophrenias. *Psychiatry* 4: 149–155.

INDEX

of borderline individual, 71-72, 100
of schizophrenic, 142
Interpretation, 194-196, 198
in expressive psychotherapy, 206-208
of projection mechanisms, 214
Interventions, 207-208
Interview
semistructured, 76
structural, 61
Introject, holding, 107-109, 210-213

Jacobson, E., 16, 32
Jonas, J., 80, 83, 119, 121
Judgment, 27

Kendell, R., 145
Kernberg, O., 16, 22, 24-26, 32, 34, 36, 37, 51, 53-67, 69-70, 76-78, 80-85, 87, 90-91, 93, 95, 102, 105-106, 117-118, 123, 128-135, 172, 184, 193, 196, 205, 210, 215
expressive psychotherapy of, 206-208
object relations theory of, 63-67
Kety, S., 79-81
Klein, D., 78-80, 120, 159, 184
Klein, M., 32, 65, 141
Klerman, G., 54, 78, 83, 119
Knight, R., xii, 42, 48-49, 51, 78, 95
Kohut, H., 18, 37, 47, 117-118, 123-135, 159, 184, 191, 196, 212
Kolb, J., 54, 75, 76, 83, 119
Kraepelin, E., 137-138, 148-149
Kris, E., 27, 32

Latent psychosis, 41, 45-46
Latent schizophrenia, 41
Levels of psychological functioning, 109-110, 118

Libidinal drive, 11
in schizophrenia, 141
Libidinal object constancy, 64-67
Lichtenberg, 22
Limit setting, 208
Lipinski, J., 13, 115, 141, 149
Lowenstein, 32

Mahler, M., 8, 59, 106, 144
developmental model of, 63-64
Major object, 109
absent, 110
frustrating, 109-110
supportive, 109
Masochism, 47
Masterson, J., xii, 98, 105-107, 109, 206
Mastery, 216
Masturbation
without fantasy, 43
repetitive, 11
Matthews, S., 146-147
McDevitt, J., 65
Medication, 80, 120, 159, 184
supplementing therapy, 201
Meissner, W., xii, 24-25, 66-67, 77-78, 87-93, 107, 117, 159, 172, 178, 184, 205
Meyers, B., 4, 50
Mirror transference, 124
Modified exploratory psychotherapy, 208-210
Mosher, L., 146-147
Mother, borderline, 106, 208

Narcissism, 46
Narcissistic line of development, 125
Narcissistic personality, 123-135
and aggressive drive, 129
analyzability of, 124-125
borderline personality and, 117-118, 130-132
DSM III diagnosis of, 132-135
fusion in, 130
healthier, 130-132